MEXICO CITY

By the staff of Editions Berlitz

Revised edition 1981

Preface

A new kind of travel guide for the jet age. Berlitz has packed all you need to know about Mexico City into this compact and colorful book, one of series on the world's top tourist areas.

Like our phrase books and dictionaries, this book fits your pocket—in size and price. It also aims to fit your travel needs:

- It concentrates on your specific destination—Mexico City.

- It combines easy reading with fast facts: what to see and do, where to shop, what to eat.

- An authoritative A-to-Z "blueprint" fills the back of the book, giving clear-cut answers to all your questions, from "Where can I find a babysitter?" to "How do I get from the airport to town?"—plus special sections on planning your budget, how to get there and when to go.

- Easy-to-read maps in full color pinpoint sights you'll want to see.

In short, this handy guide will enhance your enjoyment of Mexico City. From spectacular Aztec pyramids to the elegant shops of the Zona Rosa, from the treasures of the Museum of Anthropology to fiestas and mariachis, Berlitz tells you clearly and concisely what it's all about.

Let your travel agent help you choose a hotel.
Let a restaurant guide help you find a good place to eat.
But to decide "What should we do today?", travel with Berlitz.

How to use this guide

If time is short, look for items to visit which are printed in bold type in this book, e.g., **Palacio de Iturbide.** Those sights most highly recommended are not only given in bold type but also carry our traveler symbol, e.g., **Teotihuacán.**

Area specialist: Ken Bernstein. Photography: Claude Huber. We are most grateful to Lic. Laura Aguilar Fisch and V. M. Nicholson for their help in the preparation of this book. We also wish to thank the Mexican National Tourist Council and Terramar A.G. for their valuable assistance.

4   Cartography: Falk-Verlag, Hamburg.

Contents

Maps: Mexico City Central Area pp. 26–27, Mexico, D.F. p. 56, Excursions South p. 64, Acapulco p. 72.

Mexico City and the Mexicans

For art, archaeology and anthropology, Mexico City is a "must." But there's also plenty of action on more mundane fronts: teeming markets and chic boutiques, bullfights and nightclubs. This cosmopolitan capital is breathtaking, and not only because of the altitude—7,350 feet.

The city sprawls upon a plateau flat as a tortilla entirely surrounded by mountains and snow-capped volcanoes. This encirclement of the Valley of Mexico means that metropolitan smog is usually trapped in place, accentuating the short supply of oxygen. The prescription is to take it easy, but good advice is hard to follow when there's so much to see and do.

You'll never have time enough in the Museum of Anthropology, Mexico's incomparable collection of Indian arts and handicrafts. All the while you can study the people at first hand—those uniformed schoolchildren have the same flat-nosed faces as the ancient Indian masks and sculptures. And when archaeological remains are too large to house in a museum, they've left them where they are—like the Aztec temple at the Pino Suárez subway station, surrounded by a patio and open to the sky.

The bright, quiet subway system, called the Metro, is one of the obviously dynamic aspects of modern Mexico City. Another is the advanced architecture of skyscrapers, government buildings and housing projects all over town. But then, Mexicans have been imaginative architects for thousands of years—since the first intriguing pyramids. The innovative modern buildings contrast pleasantly with precious Spanish colonial churches and palaces. They, in turn, were built of the stones of majestic Aztec shrines demolished during the early excesses of the Conquest.

The City was founded in 1325, nearly two centuries before Cortés and his Spanish forces arrived. The Aztecs built a formidable Shangri-La called Tenochtitlán on an island in the middle of a mountain lake. They expanded the city with land fills, drainage programs and ingenious causeways. The Spanish conquerors continued the reclamation program, and natural evaporation finished

Modern buildings line Reforma, elegant boulevard in Mexico City.

6

the job. Now Mexico City is on dry land, though old buildings are perilously sinking into the spongy subsoil.

Mexican engineers have saved the cathedral from subsiding out of sight, and built earthquake-proof skyscrapers, but no one seems able to keep the city from being submerged in a flood of humanity. The population is estimated at anywhere from 10 to 15 million, a big city by any standards. And in spite of radio commercials singing, "The small family lives better," the birth rate is nearly twice as high as the world average. Add to this the relentless invasions of *paracaidistas*

(parachutists)—squatters seeking opportunity in the commercial, industrial and bureaucratic capital of the country. They arrive from the provinces at the rate of more than a thousand a day.

The city which grudgingly adopts them is called México, D.F. (Distrito Federal—federal district, with a status similar to Washington, D.C.). When Mexicans speak of "México" they may mean the city, the surrounding state of Mexico, or

Typical Siqueiros mural stands out alongside huge hotel. Opposite: piggyback expedition in Alameda.

the entire country—the United Mexican States.

Though Mexico City is about as far south as Bombay, the extreme altitude gives it a temperate climate. Aside from palm trees, the only tropical overtones are the rains, which occur almost daily between late May and early October, but only in the afternoon or evening.

The inhabitants of México, D.F. are lovable in spite of their faults. Accused of apathy, fatalism and irresponsibility, they're only punctual when it's time to quit work for the day and think nothing of littering the streets, because they know regiments of broom-and-dustpan commandos are on the way. If they have a weakness for drinking, reckless driving and fancy titles, the compensation usually is that they are friendly and kind, sometimes *too* kind. The locals will rarely correct your mistakes in Spanish, and they may even misdirect you on the street because admitting ignorance would be impolite.

The gentle people of Mexico are among the great highlights of the metropolis: the balloon salesman so well stocked he seems ready to fly away; the woman producing tortillas on a hand-operated press, while munching potato chips out of a plastic bag; the old-fashioned photographer disappearing beneath the black hood of his shoebox camera; hand-holding young couples being serenaded by the same barrel-organ great-great-grandmother listened to.

You'll remember other romantic sounds of Mexico: a mariachi band playing its heart out for a señorita; the flute of an itinerant knife-sharpener; the doleful steam whistle of the baked yam cart. And not so romantic: in Mexico City the garbage truck doesn't just arrive to the clatter of bouncing cans and lids. No, one garbage-man walks ahead of the truck, ringing a town-crier bell to proclaim the presence of his colleagues. It's protocol.

Only the pressures of time and altitude could limit your enjoyment of this great city. If you devote too much attention to the museums you may miss some of the ancient and colonial historic sites. You'll want to make time for the shrine of Guadalupe, the flowered canals of Xochimilco and the university with its startling murals. Save half a day for an excursion to Teotihuacán,

Visitors gravely pose for a photo after a visit to Guadalupe shrine.

where you can climb to the top of two of the western hemisphere's largest pyramids and survey the city plan of a lost civilization. You'll want to cram in the local color of a bullfight or jai-alai or a big soccer match. And the shopping is simply sensational—from penny trinkets to priceless antiques.

Nothing in Mexico is quite the way you anticipated—almost everything is better. Every day you'll be making memorable discoveries, as subtle as a new shade of bougainvillea or as momentous as understanding the grandeur of an ancient culture.

A Brief History

In Mexico City, history is all around you, and not only in ancient ruins and graceful colonial mansions. Look into the face of the swarthy woman squatting on the sidewalk cooking tacos over a charcoal fire. In her oriental eyes you can see the origin of Mexico's first inhabitants.

Tens of thousands of years ago, migrants from Asia walked

Faces, in a city street and in the Museum of Anthropology, tell the story of Mexico's distant origins.

across the frozen Bering Strait and worked their way down through Alaska and North America. They walked all the way to Mexico. It was a foot-slogging saga, for horses were unknown here until the 16th century, when the conquerors disembarked from Europe. (The first amazed native reaction classified a man-on-horse as a new variety of animal with 2 arms and 4 legs.)

Eventually the early Mexicans settled down to a life of farming instead of roaming and hunting. Corn was the mainstay of life—as it still is. In any market-place today you can buy a stone grinding dish and pestle for making your own tortilla flour. The design hasn't changed in centuries.

Teotihuacán

About 30 miles northeast of Mexico City you can walk the abandoned streets of Teotihuacán, a mysterious city of the golden age of pre-hispanic Mexico. About 1,500 years ago, when most European capitals were just overgrown villages, Teotihuacán may have been the biggest city in the world. The great pyramids were the heart of an advanced theocratic society. Though cut off from the mainstream of world knowledge, the Indians there

"invented" numbers, a writing system, a valid calendar and complex construction techniques.

Teotihuacán declined in the 7th century A.D.—we don't know why—and was destroyed by invaders from the north. The subsequent years led to the reign of various conflicting tribes; among them were the clever people after whom the city and country are named, the Mexicas (pronounced meh-SHEE-kas). But they are better known as Aztecs.

Rivera mural in National Palace depicts daily life in Tenochtitlán.

Tenochtitlán

For years, the legend says, the Aztecs had been wandering the Valley of Mexico in search of an improbable omen: an eagle perched on a cactus with a snake in its beak. One day in 1325 they saw this vision on an island in the middle of Lake Texcoco. There they built the city of Tenochtitlán. You can see the ruins of their temple just north of the National Palace, across the street from the cathedral—still in the middle of town, though the name has been changed from Tenochtitlán to Mexico City.

Tenochtitlán developed into a brilliant urban civilization. Aqueducts brought spring water to the center of town; you can still see part of an Aztec pipeline in the middle of Avenida Chapultepec. Elsewhere, awesome pyramids were built as a focus for religion. Prisoners-of-war, slaves and others were led to the top to be sacrificed to the gods at ceremonies attended by tens of thousands of people. The nobility—priests who performed the gory sacrificial rites and soldiers who provided the victims—lived comfortably amid works of art. Children of all classes went to school, and relays of runners brought fish from the sea to the lavish table of the emperor.

Enter Cortés

A small fleet of Spanish ships commanded by Hernán Cortés arrived at Veracruz, on the gulf coast, on Good Friday, April 21, 1519. When the news reached Tenochtitlán, the emperor Moctezuma II*, fearing Cortés incarnated the returning god, Quetzalcoatl, sent gifts to the invaders, hoping thus to buy them off. The tactic backfired. Once Cortés had seen the opulent trinkets he set out to trace their origin.

More than six months after landing on the Mexican coast the Spanish expedition got its first view of Tenochtitlán. It was breathtaking. "Like the enchantments," as a chronicler put it, "a dream." The city was bigger and more luxurious than any in Spain. The main pyramid was as tall as the tops of the cathedral spires today.

Moctezuma, in a huge green feathered head-dress and flowing robes, came to the edge of town to greet the visitors. With all deference, he invited them to stay in his father's palace on the corner of the main square (the spot now occupied by the national pawn shop). Within a matter of days Cortés repaid the hospitality by arrest-

---

* Also known as Montezuma.

15

ing the emperor and seizing control of his proud nation.

Vanquished and leaderless, the Aztecs submitted until one of the subordinates of Cortés panicked and ordered his troops to open fire on a religious ceremony. Reacting to the massacre, the Indians rebelled. The Spaniards withdrew to their palace to wait out the siege. During this time the captive Moctezuma died. The Spanish version is that he was attacked by a hostile mob of his former subjects. But Indian accounts say the Spaniards murdered him.

After a month of encirclement Cortés ordered his hungry, thirsty troops to abandon Tenochtitlán. In the desperate run to safety an estimated 400 Spanish conquerors were lost. Many, burdened with armor and loot, drowned in the canals. The disaster is known as *La Noche Triste*, the sad night.

But Cortés would not let the prize of an enchanted city escape him. He regrouped and mobilized a fifth column of rival Indian tribes with resentments against the Aztecs. Meanwhile the defenders of Tenochtitlán had been laid low by an epidemic of smallpox imported by the Spaniards.

Moctezuma's successor, the brave emperor Cuauhtémoc, tried to rally his defenses against a new Spanish attack in early 1521. But the outmanned Aztecs retreated to the northern suburbs. You can still see the ruins of the last battlefield, now called the Plaza de las Tres Culturas. Cuauhtémoc was captured, tortured and, much later, hanged. European technology, determination and greed had triumphed over Aztec civilization.

New Spain

Cortés reigned briefly as dictator over what was re-named the Kingdom of New Spain. He moved to the southern suburb of Coyoacán—still a stately old district—and ordered the center of the city demolished and rebuilt as an area for Spaniards only. The Indians were prohibited from entering what had been the sacred precinct of their faith.

Franciscan missionaries from Europe soon swarmed over the native quarters to convert the Aztecs to Christianity. This was attained within one generation, in part because the Indians were accustomed to adapting imposed religions to their own needs.

Dazzling cupolas, and red parasol, overshadow a shoebox cameraman.

What spurred the speedy and total conversion of the natives just ten years after the conquest was the strange case of Juan Diego, a simple Indian, newly baptized, who saw visions of the Virgin Mary. The bishop refused to believe him until he displayed a miraculous image imprinted on his cloak. Science has never satisfactorily explained the picture of the dark-skinned Madonna now venerated as the patron saint of Mexico. On the north side of Mexico City, on the hill where the apparition occurred, the Basilica of Our Lady of Guadalupe is one of the world's best known shrines.

Having outlawed the human sacrifices of the pagans, the Spaniards in 1596 imported the sacrifices of the Inquisition to New Spain. Archbishop Pedro Moya de Contreras officiated

History lesson: Juan O'Gorman mural in Chapultepec Castle hails heroes of independence struggle.

at what is now the western edge of the Alameda park as the condemned were burned at the stake.

Revolution and Turmoil

Spain sent Mexico a long line of viceroys—many of them inept, cruel or corrupt—to rule the mixed population, but absentee ownership of Mexico's riches engendered resentment. As life became more cosmopolitan, revolutionary ideas crept in from abroad.

In 1810 an old priest, Miguel Hidalgo, led a conspiracy which liberated political prisoners and locked up the colonial authorities in their stead. From his church in the village called Dolores he proclaimed: *"Mexicanos, ¡Viva México!"* "The Cry of Dolores" inspired an irregular army of rebels in a doomed struggle against the might of the Spanish empire. Captured, defrocked and executed, Hidalgo became the first of the great Mexican hero-martyrs.

His successor at the head of the revolutionary movement was another priest, José María Morelos, who convened a congress in 1813 which formally declared independence from Spain. Though he was a better military leader than Hidalgo, Morelos suffered the same fate—execution before a Spanish firing squad.

But the popular movement became impossible to check, and Spain finally granted Mexico its independence in 1821. The insurgent military leader, Colonel Agustín de Iturbide, not only won control of the first independent government, he crowned himself Emperor of Mexico in the following year. Predictably, he soon began ruling as a dictator. But after only ten months he was **19** forced to abdicate. Iturbide sailed to exile, returning about a year later, unaware that congress had condemned him to death in his absence. Like so many Mexican historical figures, the dethroned emperor died before the firing squad.

The military leader who prompted Iturbide's abdication, General Antonio López de Santa Anna, took over the presidency himself in 1833. It was the first of several terms in office — alternating with spells of exile — for one of the most colorful characters ever to rule any country. With flair and eccentricity this complicated man often got Mexico into trouble and occasionally out of it. He declared his birthday a national holiday and styled himself "His Most Supreme Highness." Aside from titles and medals, he was mainly interested in roulette and cockfights. Turmoil and disaster enveloped his era.

Santa Anna was the general whose troops slaughtered the Texan rebels holding out in San Antonio's Alamo. In the revenge battle of San Jacinto, General Sam Houston wiped out the Mexicans; Santa Anna was captured and held until he signed a paper recognizing the independence of Texas.

In the War of 1847 Santa Anna was again on the losing side. A strong American expeditionary force led by General Winfield Scott marched from Veracruz to Mexico City. The only Mexican heroes were a unit of army cadets, holed up in Chapultepec Castle. After three hopeless days, the surviving "boy heroes" leaped to their deaths shouting patriotic slogans. The invaders carried on marching to the National Palace. In the resulting Treaty of Guadalupe, a desperately defeated Mexico handed over Texas, New Mexico, Arizona and California to the new conquerors.

Juárez and Maximilian

Benito Juárez, a Zapotec Indian, began life as a shepherd before becoming a lawyer, congressman, governor and president. He inaugurated the sweeping reform laws (among them, separation of church and state) after which Mexico City's most fashionable boulevard, Paseo de la Reforma, was named. He served two terms as president — before and after the bizarre interlude of the Hapsburg connection.

In 1864, for a whole series of complicated political reasons, Napoleon III installed the elegant Maximilian, Archduke of Austria as ruler of Mexico.

Supported by a full-scale French army of occupation and the scheming of local conservatives, the somewhat naïve red-bearded emperor ruled as well as he knew how. But the brief imperial era is most remembered for the glamour of life at Chapultepec Castle, which the emperor's beautiful wife Charlotte* (daughter of the Belgian king) turned into the party capital of the hemisphere. When France withdrew its support, the surreal episode ended. Charlotte, politicking for her husband in Europe at the time, went mad, and Maximilian was executed by firing squad on June 19, 1867.

Into the 20th Century

Porfirio Díaz, another of the soldier-politicians, ruled Mexico as dictator or, alternately, power behind the throne for more than 30 years. So massive was his impact that the epoch which finally ended in 1911 is known as the *Porfiriato*. Though usually portrayed as a villain, Díaz can be given credit for overseeing the country's most ambitious economic expansion.

The revolution which ultimately overturned Díaz was waged, among others, by the glamorous guerilla fighters Pancho Villa and Emiliano Zapata. The leader of the six-month struggle, a well-to-do politician named Francisco Madero, was swept to power as Díaz hurried to exile in Paris. But in 1913, a sinister general, Victoriano Huerta, arrested Madero and arranged for him to be murdered. The United States embassy was charged with collusion.

Huerta quickly took over as president-dictator. In 1914 the United States turned against him and in a bit of classic gunboat diplomacy, the U.S. Marines occupied Veracruz. Mexicans bitterly remember the battle as the Veracruz Massacre. Within three months General Huerta had indeed fallen; he grabbed all the portable assets of the national treasury and sailed to exile.

Historic legislation

The long-running Mexican revolution has left some memorable monuments of reform. The 1917 constitution, for instance, included a bill of rights for the Mexican worker, a minimum wage, an eight-hour day and the right to strike. This is all contained in Article 123 (which is commemorated in the street of the same name in the center of Mexico City).

---

* Also known as Carlota.

In 1924 the congress cracked down on the Catholic Church — reflecting years of divided feelings among laymen and politicians. Congress forbade priests to teach in elementary schools, to speak against the constitution or even to wear their cassocks in public. This law theoretically remains in force — notice the absence of priests on the streets — but the Mexicans still go to church and usually disregard old resentments.

President Lázaro Cárdenas, who ruled from 1934 to 1940, fathered many agrarian and economic reform acts, including one of the most drastic in Mexico's history — the expropriation of foreign oil companies. For this he's considered a national hero, and perhaps the inspiration for takeovers in other countries many years later. In the 1970s Mexico's home-owned oil resources were discovered to be vastly bigger, and more vital, than Cárdenas could have imagined.

Even with this and other natural wealth, the modern history of Mexico has been a struggle: a devastating foreign debt, a worrisomely high birth rate, squatters crowding the cities in cruel poverty. The authorities hope that the devaluation and subsequent floating of the peso will enhance exports and tourism, that tax reform will level out some injustices, that the traditional corruption will be curbed, and that industry can provide jobs so that hundreds of thousands of desperate Mexicans don't have to smuggle themselves across the Rio Grande. The Mexican revolution goes on.

Local Lingo

So many Spanish words are different in Mexico that one dictionary of *Mejicanismos* runs to nearly 1,200 pages. Many Mexican words are imaginative. Here are a few, with a literal translation and then the figurative, Mexican meaning:

aviador — aviator — a bureaucrat who never works but "flies in" twice a month to pick up his pay

coyote — a species of wolf — a wheeler-dealer, often operating on the street

mordida — a bite — a bribe, graft

paracaidista — parachutist — squatter who swoops down onto someone's property to seize it

tecolote — an owl — a policeman

Statue in the Reforma honors the last Aztec emperor, Cuauhtémoc.

What to See

Arriving for the first time in a city this big, it's worthwhile joining a guided tour to get your bearings. Then you can carry on exploring as you wish by taxi, bus or Metro—the Mexico City subway is an experience in itself. The best sightseeing is always afoot, and most of the following sections are so arranged that you can organize easy walking tours for yourself. We don't recommend that you drive yourself in the city—the hair-raising traffic and the problems of triple-parking might interfere with the pleasure of your vacation.

You'll soon discover that the main north-south artery of Mexico City is called Insurgentes and the grand boulevard going northeast-southwest is Paseo de la Reforma. This handsome avenue, often likened to Paris' Champs-Elysées, runs from Chapultepec Park through the main tourist area and past the edge of the downtown Alameda Park. But the heart of the metropolis is a mile east of Alameda, in the exact spot from which Moctezuma directed his empire.

The Zócalo

The main square of Mexico City, the Zócalo, calls to mind Moscow's Red Square: immense, faced by forbidding buildings steeped in history, and crowded with provincial peasants and worldly tourists. But while the ancient cobbles of Red Square are for pedestrians only, traffic roars around the edge of the Zócalo. In the center of the great plaza stands a solitary flagpole.

Zócalo means pedestal or

Spaniards designed vast plaza as Mexico's main square, the Zócalo.

24

base. A monument to Mexican independence was to have been erected here but the project never got off the ground. Though the official name is Plaza de la Constitución, the name "Zócalo" is most often used. And, in fact, the main square of every town in Mexico is now known informally as the Zócalo.

When the Spanish conquerors seized the city, they destroyed the Temple Court of the Aztecs and built this plaza just to the south of it. Here they established a flourishing marketplace, which was cleared on occasion for the earliest bullfights in New Spain. Another spectacle was the public execution of prisoners, the gallows were right here.

The entire east side of the Zócalo is filled by the enormous **Palacio Nacional** (National Palace). Here, the President of Mexico and other officials maintain their offices. You can walk right in through

MEXICO CITY
CENTRAL AREA

ZONA ROSA

1 Museo Nacional de Antropología
2 Galería de Historia
3 Museo de Arte Moderno
4 Monumento a los Niños Héroes
5 Fuente de Diana Cazadora
6 Monumento a la Independencia
7 Mercado de Londres

8 Monumento a Cuauhtémoc
9 Monumento a la Revolución
10 Museo de San Carlos
11 El Caballito
12 Pinacoteca Virreinal
13 Mercado Ciudadela
14 Mercado de San Juan

the central gateway, which reveals a huge three-story arcaded patio. Turn left and walk a few steps to the ceremonial staircase, which is decorated with memorable **murals**

Long lens compresses expanse of National Palace. Right: balancing newspapers on a delivery bicycle.

by Diego Rivera. They illustrate the history of Mexico from old Indian legends to the 20th century; in his art you'll notice Rivera often links contemporary events with incidents from the Conquest. Along the left staircase you can see the portraits of such economic wizards as J. P. Morgan,

Cornelius Vanderbilt, John D. Rockefeller, Jr. ...and Karl Marx. (Excursion guides warn their clients not to look up at the murals too long lest dizziness ensue; at this altitude rubbernecking can have its perils.) This palace, rebuilt several times over several centuries, is thought to have been among the very first buildings of the capital of New Spain.

Only a block to the north you get a quick idea of the earlier history of the city. At the corner of Guatemala and Seminario streets you'll see the **ruins** of the main Aztec temple to Tlaloc and Huitzilopóchtli, gods of the rain and war.

Curiously, this archaeological treasure-trove went undiscovered until 1913. From the sidewalk you can look down upon the vestiges of four levels of a major pyramid. When compared with other archaeological discoveries in Mexico this is unexceptional, but the location —in the very heart of Mexico City—makes the building blocks and stone sculptures quite fascinating. The major find, an enormous statue of an Aztec god, can be seen only on Saturday mornings. Other artefacts are displayed in the Museo de las Culturas (see p. 62).

The **Metropolitan Cathedral** and the adjoining, richly baroque parish church tilt apart dizzily. Because of the tricky terrain, all the old churches of the city lean precariously, their doorways often far below street level. To save the cathedral, hundreds of supports were sunk 130 feet into the ground. By the end of 1975, engineers declared the building secure.

The conquerors established their first cathedral in 1525 but the building was considered too modest for the capital of New Spain. In its stead the present cathedral was begun, based on 16th-century plans. The Sagrario (sanctuary) next door is an 18th-century afterthought.

The richness of the stone carvings on the exterior of the cathedral is equalled by the grandiose effects inside. A big fire more than a decade ago destroyed many of the glories of the interior but they are being meticulously restored.

There are seven chapels on each side of the nave. You'll notice an unusual sacred image in a chapel on the right—a black figure of Christ crucified, known as *El Señor del Veneno* (Our Lord of the Poison). According to legend, someone tried to murder a local bishop by putting poison on this figure. But when the bishop knelt to kiss the feet of Christ, the statue shrivelled from the poison, turned black and the bishop was miraculously saved.

To the west of the cathedral is a stately building worth seeing for historical and con-

Baptism in Sagrario, adjoining the Cathedral. Building tilts due to subsidence in the spongy subsoil.

Street Names

In Mexico City the name of a street often tells you where to find it.

Many neighborhoods name their streets according to a particular theme. Thus in the Pink Zone the streets commemorate great cities from Belgrade and Berlin to Varsovia and Venecia (Warsaw and Venice). On the opposite side of Paseo de la Reforma the streets are named for rivers, including the Amazon and the Mississippi. One district's streets impartially honor communist leaders—Marx, Trotsky and José Stalin.

But the authorities eventually ran out of ideas and hundreds of outlying streets have numbers instead of names.

temporary reasons. In this spot was the Aztec palace in which Cortés and his army were housed as guests of the emperor in 1519, and where Moctezuma was killed. In the 18th century the **Monte de Piedad** (National Pawnshop) was established here. Today this institution continues to lend money to the poor, and not so poor, with personal property as security. Unredeemed items are auctioned or sold over the counter. This would be a prime location for a department store, and in fact with all the

TV sets, refrigerators and jewelry for sale it looks like one. The antique department would normally attract tourists, but experts say the really valuable things are skimmed by the professionals. On the sidewalk outside, notice the touts—called *coyotes*—offering quicker money to prospective pawnshop customers.

This historic center of town has a high concentration of evocative old buildings. If you have the time, stroll three blocks north from the pawnshop to **Plaza de Santo Domingo.** Suddenly you're in Old Spain, in a provincial square, decaying but intriguing. Under the arches sit old-fashioned public scribes, now equipped with typewriters. They fill out government forms, translate documents and even write love letters for illiterate or bashful clients. If the correspondence should lead to the altar, any of the printers with hand presses set up here can run off the wedding invitations while you wait.

From Zócalo to Alameda Park

Four blocks west of the Zócalo, at Avenida Madero 17, you can cash your travelers' checks in a palace. The **Palacio de Iturbide,** home of Mexico's first emperor, is one of the richest baroque buildings in the capital—and not only because it now houses a bank. The restored patio is simply magnificent. Notice the stone-carving on the capitals of the columns and the gargoyles.

One block farther west, look carefully for the **Iglesia de San Francisco** (St. Francis' church). Just next door to a more modern church, it has sunk so deeply into the soft soil that the entrance, set far back from the street, is now at cellar level. The intricately carved facade is a landmark. Franciscan monks founded this church in the first years of the Spanish occupation, but the present structure is the third to be built on the site.

Across the street, you can't miss the dazzling **Casa de los Azulejos** (House of Tiles). What might have been a folly is one

Professional scribe ghost-writes a letter on an ancient typewriter.

of the most pleasant and distinctive buildings in Mexico. The exterior of this 16th-century palace is entirely covered in Puebla tiles (dating from the early 18th century). Inside, the palace has been converted into a restaurant, soda fountain, souvenir store and pharmacy. Diners in the beautiful main patio are usually unaware of its dramatic history: on the monumental staircase an early owner of the palace, a Count of Orizaba, was murdered by the swain of one of his daughters; later the young man was hanged from the balcony. *Bon appetit!*

Tour guides jokingly call the **Torre Latinoamericana** (Latin American Tower) the highest, if not the tallest, skyscraper in the world; the ground floor is a mile and a half above sea level. In traditional Latin cities the church towers tell the time but in Mexico City the top of this building provides the hour, minute and second in a big digital display. From the 42nd floor (small entry charge) a spiral staircase ascends to the roof. On a normal day the edges of the city fade into the

In land of unpunctuality, clock on skyscraper flashes seconds. Right: Bellas Artes mural by Siqueiros.

smog, but with luck you may see some of the distant mountains. Inside the tower a diploma is displayed congratulating the architects and engineers of this cleverly designed skyscraper, which a major earthquake in 1957 left unscathed.

The **Palacio de Bellas Artes** (Fine Arts Palace), begun in 1904, took 30 years to construct, which accounts for the mixture of styles. The interior is the ultimate in 1920's *art déco*, a precursor of New York's Radio City Music Hall. By coincidence, on the third floor you can see Diego Rivera's own copy of a mural he painted in Rockefeller Center in 1933. It was destroyed by the Rockefeller management when the artist refused to delete the face of Lenin from a vignette. Notice Marx and Trotsky, as well. Other fine murals by Rivera, Orozco and Siqueiros also decorate this palace. But, unfortunately, they're only

visible in the daytime. In the evenings, when the opera house is in use for concerts or shows, the mural areas are closed.

Before visiting Alameda park, walk east along Tacuba Street to the Plaza de Minería. The chivalrous horseman on **El Caballito**—"the little horse"— is, in fact, King Charles IV of Spain, who reigned from 1788 to 1808. The statue was cast when Mexico was still a Spanish possession. After the revolution it was sarcastically called the Trojan Horse and moved to progressively less important locations.

Alameda Central, Mexico City's central park, is smack in the middle of the downtown district. The area is said to have been drained from the lake in the 16th century to provide room for maneuver for the Spanish soldiers, wary of Indian attack. It became the first city park in the early 17th century, though admission was limited to the upper classes. Official documents show that the police were ordered to bar "coarsely dressed people, barefoot beggars or nude or indecent people." After Mexican independence the Alameda became a totally public park and it remains a happy, picturesque place—a carnival of balloon sellers, ice-cream and children.

Across Avenida Juárez from the park, in the lobby of the Hotel del Prado, you can rest your feet while you study a most topical Rivera **mural,** *A Dream of a Sunday Afternoon in the Alameda Park*. This grand work—socialist realism without boredom—was painted in 1947–48.

Paseo de la Reforma

The key intersection of Avenida Juárez and Paseo de la Reforma is one of the sports where *El Caballito* once stood.

Now menacing ranks of cars and buses roar down the wide avenue in a haze of noise and fumes.

The tall white modern building across the street is the supreme headquarters of all

Fresh flowers in brilliant array struggle with traffic fumes on Reforma.

those salesmen waving lottery tickets at you on every street. Every Tuesday and Friday at 8 p.m. the public is invited to watch the numbers as they are drawn here. The next morning the winning statistics are published in the newspapers and displayed at every lottery stand, printed on cloth instead of paper for better fingering. The lottery is run for the benefit of the government's welfare program.

Beyond this palace of change is a gaudy monument that looks like an eccentric design for a dirigible hangar. A legislative mansion was to have been built here but the project was abandoned. Rather than demolish the half-finished structure, they salvaged the arches and dome and called it the Revolution Monument.

Back to the Reforma, the boulevard named for the reform movement which culminated in Mexico's 1857 constitution. This elegant avenue, with some outstanding modern buildings, is the preferred address for airline offices, smart hotels, restaurants, galleries and cultural institutions. Two of Reforma's finest new structures are the embassies of the U.S.A. and Japan. The plan for the boulevard originated with Emperor Maximilian, whose carriage could thus be driven directly and pleasantly from home (Chapultepec Castle) to the office (the National Palace).

Street scenes on Reforma: girl at handicrafts stand; buildings show generation gap in city architecture.

Monuments are planted in most of the *glorietas* (traffic circles) along the Reforma. At Reforma and Insurgentes, the last of the Aztec emperors, Cuauhtémoc, is honored in a heroic statue—feathered headdress, spear and all. Down the avenue, the tallest of the monuments is known locally as the Angel. Formally it's the Independence Monument.

The stretch of Reforma between these two monuments constitutes the northern border of an unofficial district called the **Zona Rosa** (Pink Zone). This is a fashionable new center for shopping and dining, a worldly neighborhood that is lively night and day. Many of the policemen on duty in the Pink Zone wear special badges identifying them as linguists, so visiting tourists stand little chance of getting lost here.

The long, straight trajectory of Paseo de la Reforma ends (or begins) at the entrance to Chapultepec Park. The statue of the Roman goddess Diana near here is not only beautiful but appropriate. The huntress would have been right at home in these old woods before they became the breathing space of a crowded city.

Sunday in the Pink Zone: a painter waiting for patrons of the arts.

Chapultepec Park

The first official known to have devoted himself to the beautification of El Bosque de Chapultepec (the Chapultepec Woods) was the Emperor Moctezuma II. The Aztecs provided the name, meaning "grasshopper hill" evidently because of the shape of the park's bluff. The conquering Cortés took personal custody of the park, along with other lands, but in 1530 Chapultepec became a city park. Today it's the most visited park in the republic; every weekend hundreds of thousands of people—mostly city dwellers craving trees, grass and fresh air—fan out over its lakes and fields, woods and walks.

But you didn't come all the way to Mexico for picnic possibilities. The greatest attractions of Chapultepec Park are its museums, and the undisputed champion of Mexican museums is on the right side of the continuation of Reforma through the park. The **Museo Nacional de Antropología** (National Anthropology Museum) is a knockout by any standards —a museum where nobody could possibly be bored. If ancient burial customs don't thrill you, then the jewelry or music, textiles or courtship rituals of the peoples of Mexico—or the inspired architecture of the museum itself—will more than compensate.

That stone **monolith** on the side of the road outside the museum is a representation of the rain god Tlaloc. Like 98 per cent of the items inside the museum, it's original. Only objects which might perish in the atmosphere are shown in replica. When Tlaloc was transported, with enormous difficulty, from the archaeological site to the museum, the skies opened with the heaviest rainstorm in local memory.

Once inside the museum, which is deployed around a great patio with a most original inverted fountain, you ought to begin with a guided tour. They leave about ten times a day for English speakers, less frequently in Spanish, French and German. The tours generally touch only two or three of the ten halls each devoted to an ancient civilization. But the official guide will provide a valuable introduction to Mexican history and to the museum itself, whereupon you can concentrate on the aspects that interest you most.

Among the most unforgettable items on display:

The so-called Aztec Calendar Stone from the 15th century, **41**

a 24-ton puzzle (now solved) reproduced in miniature in every souvenir shop in the country; a bone carved more than 10,000 years ago to resemble the head of a coyote; and a vase ingeniously cut from obsidian in the form of a monkey—a "late post-classic" triumph of the Aztecs.

One small problem: all the signs and legends are printed in Spanish only. Helpful hint: *III s. a.C.* means third century B.C.; *X s. d.C.*, 10th century A.D. Various illustrated guidebooks are sold at the museum's well-stocked bookstore.

After you've seen the ancient artifacts of, say, the Mayas or the Toltecs, it's fascinating to go upstairs. On the floor above each cultural hall are displays showing how the present-day descendants still live in isolated villages. These exhibits are often thronged with provincial visitors searching for their roots.

Admission charges are lower on Sundays. Guided tours in Spanish are free; for foreign languages a small sum is charged. See p. 115 for opening hours.

What to do in Chapultepec Park: have a picnic on the grass, or visit famed Museum of Anthropology.

Returning to the park's main entrance, the monument with six marble columns in a semi-circle honors Mexico's *niños héroes*—"boy heroes." These were the teen-age cadets who died heroically during the American invasion of 1847 (see p. 20). Dominating the ensemble is a sculptural group, the motherland portrayed with one dead son in her arms, another alive and ready for combat.

The **Museo de Arte Moderno** (Modern Art Museum) just to the right provides an enlightening and heartwarming survey of recent Mexican painting and sculpture. The building nearest

the "boy heroes" monument is dedicated to temporary exhibitions, while a larger structure (the main entrance is on Reforma) covers such artists as Rivera, Siqueiros and O'Gorman. One hall is devoted to the classic 19th-century Mexican landscapes of José María Velasco. There is also an exhibition of avant-garde trends in Mexican art. The two buildings are separated by a small park with trees, flowers, grass, powerful statues and giant mobiles. The architecture, based on the perfection of the circle, is

Near monument to "boy heroes," a display of sidewalk salesmanship.

Walls of Protest

Although the nation's three top muralists spent many years abroad, their work is unmistakably Mexican.

DIEGO RIVERA (1886–1957), called the greatest modern master of fresco painting, created powerful images with a message that all could understand. A Communist for 50 years, he dramatized the class struggle from the Aztecs to Stalin.

JOSÉ CLEMENTE OROZCO (1883–1949) was often abroad, so most of his work is on foreign walls. But some of his cruelly uncompromising murals may be seen in the Fine Arts Palace and Chapultepec Castle.

DAVID ALFARO SIQUEIROS (1898–1974) suffered prison and exile for his radical politics. His three-dimensional innovations and striking colors distinguish the last of the 20th-century titans.

original and impressive. Credit goes to the same man who designed the Anthropology Museum, Pedro Ramírez Vázquez.

See p. 114 for museum hours.

From here it's a 15 minute walk uphill to the **Castillo de Chapultepec** (Chapultepec Castle). A tunnel dug into the bottom of the hillside leads to an elevator, but a crowd of non-climbers is usually waiting in a hopelessly long line. Whichever way you surmount "grasshopper hill," you're in for a pleasant combination of history and art—and a superb view over Mexico City. This was the home of Maximilian and Charlotte, and you can see their regally furnished quarters. Part of the castle has been turned into a history museum—the Museo Nacional de Historia. You can take a guided tour through halls filled with historic objects and paintings. There are gripping historic murals by Siqueiros and O'Gorman. In the Sala de Banderas (flag hall), a sentry, immobile but for his eyes, stands guard with a modern automatic rifle over historic banners and battle flags.

Hours of admission to Chapultepec Castle are listed on p. 114. A modest entry fee is charged.

A hundred yards from the castle, the **Galería de Historia** is another architectural brainstorm by Ramírez Vázquez. This snail-shaped glass building snuggles into the hillside. You enter at the top and walk downhill through displays of Mexican history since independence in 1810. See a toy soldier army of U.S. invaders

45

besieging Chapultepec Castle and paintings or re-creations of other often bloody events of the 19th and 20th centuries. The last hall is a chapel-like retreat with sunlight streaming through the high dome onto a dramatic sculpture of the national eagle-and-snake symbol.

Admission to the gallery is free. See p. 114 for hours.

At the bottom of the hill, a cheerful surprise awaits the traveler who has plodded through enough museums for the day. Audiorama is a small circular tropical park in which you can slump in a comfortable chair, close your eyes and let recorded classical music sweep over you from hi-fi stereo speakers—and it's free.

Nearby are some of the surviving *ahuehuete* trees, hundreds of years old. They're members of an endangered species; the climate has changed over the centuries and a major conservation effort is aimed at keeping these cypress-like veterans alive.

The **Chapultepec Park Zoo** claims to be the first in the world, founded before anyone in Europe got the idea of putting live animals on display. The educational innovation is credited to the Emperor Moctezuma, around the year 1500. There are 2,000 species of birds, reptiles and mammals on show; you can see many of them briefly from a scenic railway. Children will also be interested in the small lakes, where rowboats for rent share the water with a fleet of swans. And a big amusement park within Chapultepec is known for its roller-coaster *(Montaña Rusa)*. For smaller children a separate amusement park has rides and other things to do.

Three more sights in Chapultepec Park are typically Mexican. The Fountain of Netzahualcóyotl is a very long ensemble carved in gray stone honoring a great Indian chief. The Fountain of the Gods, also of extravagant dimensions, features a row of ancient Indian idols. Finally, at the municipal waterworks in the park, Diego Rivera constructed a sprawling sculpture dedicated to Tlaloc, the rain god. Sprays of water shoot from the recumbent god's forehead, each of his toenails is the size of a TV screen. This one-of-a-kind pagan tribute, surrounded by brilliant flowerbeds, is grotesquely glorious.

Two more museums in the park, of special interest to children, are listed on p. 62.

Look-alikes: a schoolgirl stands before Chapultepec Castle mural.

Tlatelolco and Guadalupe

On the north side of the city, just over a mile from the Zócalo, stones bring to life the history of Mexico. The **Plaza de las Tres Culturas** (Plaza of the Three Cultures) at Tlatelolco is the site of the last Aztec battle. A plaque on the spot tells the story simply but movingly: "The 13th of August, 1521, heroically defended by Cuauhtémoc, Tlatelolco fell under the control of Hernán Cortés. It was neither a triumph nor a defeat. It was the painful birth of the mixed-race people which is the Mexico of today."

Here you can see the outlines of an elaborate, logically laid-out Aztec city center. Above these ruins stands a typical Spanish colonial church of the early 16th century. It's immediately obvious that the church is built of stones from the neighboring Indian shrine

which was torn down. In the plaza alongside the church, decendants of Cuauhtémoc and Cortés skate, ride bikes, run and play. The area is called Plaza of the Three Cultures because of the conjunction here of important pre-Columbian and Spanish structures as well as contemporary Mexican buildings, most notably the marble skyscraper of the foreign ministry.

A short distance east of the plaza, in a government housing project (population 70,000), an old colonial convent has been restored to house a 1944 mural by Siqueiros showing the final struggle of Cuauhtémoc against the myth of Spanish invincibility.

The patron saint of Mexico, and of Latin America, is the Virgin of Guadalupe. Her **shrine,** 2½ miles north of Tlate-

Aztec, Spanish, Mexican history converge at site of final battle. Opposite: fun in hall of mirrors.

lolco, is one of the world's great religious centers. Since the miraculous apparition in 1531 (see p. 18) five basilicas have been built in succession. The latest — an ultramodern concrete and marble structure shaped like a volcano — is a cavernous church with only one icon. There are no statues or paintings, just a single relic — the portrait of the dark-skinned Virgin Mary mysteriously imprinted on 16th-century cloth.

To replace the graceful old basilica that is subsiding into the treacherous soil across the plaza, the new church has room for 20,000 people. An underpass near the altar permits visitors to get a good look at the revered image without blocking the view of the worshippers on the main floor. You'll be impressed by the crowds who come to pray here. Many of them are simple country folk who cover the last stage of the pilgrimage on their knees. But the Virgin of Guadalupe means something special to all the people; even the most sophisticated Mexican is likely to keep a small replica of the Virgin at home.

Pilgrimage to Guadalupe: prayers at scene of miraculous apparition.

Pyramids

The word to describe **Teotihuacán** is "awesome." This holy city, little more than an hour's drive north of Mexico City, flourished nearly 2,000 years ago. And then it died — we're not sure how or when. And centuries later the Aztecs came upon it, discovering accidentally that beneath those steep grassy hills were magnificent pyramids. The Aztecs gave this ghostly city the name Teotihuacán—"place where men become gods." And they named the Pyramid of the Sun and the Pyramid of the Moon, and the Avenue of the Dead, which is laid out on an incredibly accurate north-south axis. We don't know what these monuments were called by those who built them and worshipped here, nor the name of the ancient culture which had a system of numbers, hieroglyphics and used a calendar.

A small museum on the edge of the site has models of the pyramids and replicas of works of art found there. (The originals are mostly to be seen in the Museum of Anthropology in Mexico City.) But there's no substitute for walking the ground here, through the vast Ciudadela (citadel) and up the steps to the top of the Pyramid of the Sun. If you're reasonably healthy and not in a rush you'll be rewarded by the climb. Wild mountain flowers grow in the narrow strips of earth between the ageless stones, and from the summit you can see the expanse of town-planning of this ceremonial center. And you look at other sharp hills covered with grass and underbrush and wonder what may lie beneath. And even if a mountaineering souvenir salesman should offer to sell you a trinket while you're communing with mysterious forces, you'll never forget where you bought the "genuine" hand-made relics gently forced on you by one of the highest salesmen in the world.

All tour companies run guided excursions to the pyramids. If you're driving, you will pay modest fees for the toll (*cuota*) road, then again for car and passengers on entering the archaeological zone. Visiting hours: 8 a.m. to 5 p.m. A sound and light show is presented nightly except during the rainy season.

A perfect stop on your way back to Mexico City is the former Augustinian **monastery of Acolman,** now a museum. Alongside the fortress-like church is an unexpectedly ex- **51** tensive complex through which you can wander at will. You'll see how the monks lived in their cells in the 16th century. Notice the many "hidden" passages. Aside from old religious art and a collection of indigenous sculpture, you'll enjoy the cloister with its orange trees and chirping birds.

Acolman monastery is on the "free" *(libre)* road between Teotihuacán and Mexico City. Open 10 a.m. to 6 p.m.

A mysterious society lived round Teotihuacán pyramids. Below: tiny statue at Acolman monastery.

♟ University City and Suburbs

Mexico's famous University (*Universidad Nacional Autónoma de México*) is much too big to get to know in one outing: the campus covers nearly 3 square miles. But the absolutely essential sights — buildings of prime artistic and architectural interest — are close together.

The best known university building is the "windowless" **library.** This ten-story structure was designed and decorated by Juan O'Gorman, the celebrated Mexican architect and artist. (His father emigrated from Ireland to Mexico; his mother, of Irish descent, was born in Mexico.) O'Gorman covered the library's walls with millions of tiny stones of varied natural colors arranged to illustrate the history of knowledge — from Aztec astronomical signs to modern impressions of mo-

lecular structure. Although there are no windows in the stacks in which the books are stored, the reading rooms do offer natural light.

Nearby, La Torre de la Rectoría (Rector's Tower) is the administration building, where university officials attempt to keep track of well over 200,000 students. This building is emblazoned with a three-dimensional Siqueiros mural.

Here in the center of the campus, as everywhere in Mexico, it's the people who are so fascinating. In the shadow of these innovative buildings, country women with long black pigtails set up stoves and pushcarts and sell the students tacos and tropical fruit.

The university sports stadium, across the main road, is distinguished by a vast **relief** designed by Diego Rivera. For the 1968 Olympics the stadium was expanded to seat more than 100,000 people.

The present University City was begun in 1953 but the institution traces its history back to a decree of Charles V in 1551. Classes began two years later in a house just a couple of blocks from the Zócalo.

With its magnificent labs and institutes, museums and observatory, the new campus sweeps across a zone of Mexico City covered with a thick layer of volcanic rock, called *pedregal*.

El Pedregal is the name of a luxurious suburb on the opposite side of Insurgentes from the university. It's enlightening to drive through this section in which the petrified lava has been used structurally and dec-

Spontaneous elation of sports fans shows a spirited side of local life. **55**

MEXICO, D.F.

oratively to great effect. Not only are the residents obviously wealthy but many of them have used their money to build modern palaces of exquisite taste. However, you'll see the occasional ostentatious home with works of art overflowing into the garage and more swimming pools than anyone really needs. The name of the architect is generally inscribed on the facade of each house, a custom which filters down to some rather humble bungalows in other parts of Mexico City.

Two more southern suburbs are worth a look:

Coyoacán was where Cortés set up housekeeping after the conquest. The house in which he may have lived has undergone many reconstructions, but other 16th-century houses have been nicely preserved. Behind a seemingly modest facade you may glimpse a classic Spanish patio.

San Angel is a neighborhood of narrow cobbled streets with a small-town atmosphere. In the San Jacinto convent, magenta bougainvillea climbs almost to the belfry of the 16th-century church. Every Saturday morning San Angel is swamped with shoppers patronizing the *tianguis* (native market), the chic shops and the Bazaar Sábado (see p. 84).

Special on Sunday

The garden of art, **El Jardín del Arte** (also known as Sullivan Park) is on the opposite side of Reforma from the Pink Zone. Six days a week it's like any other neighborhood park —a grassy haven for baby-carriages, young cyclists and sunsoaking pensioners. But on Sunday the name of the park explains itself. Scores of professional artists arrive from near and far to set up shop, displaying their paintings for the critical judgment of their peers and for sale to visiting collectors. Many tourist buses start their Sunday excursions here. If you don't feel like buying, it's still a good occasion for taking pictures of the pictures and the artists. If you do buy a painting, you can have it wrapped for shipment at a professional packing desk thoughtfully set up in the park.

Flea Market. Sunday morning is bargain time at Lagunilla Market, just east of the Reforma at the José Martí equestrian statue (Calle Rayón). Collectors of off-beat antiques, or just junk, will be thrilled at the scope of this enormous street bazaar. You can buy pistol-holsters, seashells, plastic flowers, used toys, wind-up gramophones, live dogs, dead sparkplugs, primitive sewing machines, brass spittoons...the list is endless. A carnival atmosphere enhances the fun. But heed two warnings: never pay what the vendor originally asks, as bargaining over the price is part of the game. And above all be on the alert for pickpockets in the carefree crush.

Gondola named Conchita welcomes gringos to Xochimilco, where even the music is afloat.

While you're there, have a look inside the buildings containing the formal Lagunilla market. Hundreds of small businesses are jammed together. This is where ordinary Mexicans go to buy economical clothing, furniture and pots and pans.

Xochimilco. "Mexico's Venice" is the half-serious unofficial name for this network of canals through fertile farmland on the southern extremity of the capital. Every Sunday

the excursion buses descend on Xochimilco (from the Indian word *xochitl*, flower), but this remains essentially a Mexican scene, unspoiled by all the attention. Whole families charter gondolas and proceed to consume their picnics. The gondoliers (about 300 professionals live in Xochimilco) propel and steer their boats with long poles, deftly avoiding most collisions. Smaller canoes ply the turbid waters selling flowers, fruit baskets, hot snacks, souvenirs and even entertainment! Boatloads of mariachi or marimba musicians glide past, auditioning; if you want a serenade they'll travel in tandem. Or you can have your picture taken by a floating photographer.

The cheerfully decorated gondolas have room for about eight people around a picnic table. A two-hour trip through the good-natured traffic jams means plenty of fun for family and friends at little expense.

Your busy *remero* (gondolier) amply deserves a small tip. (Less affluent visitors cram aboard *pesero* boats, the floating equivalent of third-class buses, and have as much fun as the rich.)

Xochimilco, which has been a center of flower cultivation for 500 years, has a lively public

market you might like to investigate before or after your cruise. In addition to mouth-watering fruit and vegetables, it's strong on handicrafts and the freshest flowers.

If you're using public transportation, take the Metro to its southern terminal, Tasqueña. It's a 15 or 20 minute bus ride from there.

Bullfights. Spain's *fiesta brava* took firm root in Mexico hundreds of years ago. Sunday afternoon is the traditional time; the place is Plaza México, the world's largest bullring, holding up to 50,000 people. It's just off Insurgentes Sur, halfway between the city center and the university. You can usually buy tickets through your hotel or any of the travel agencies which run tours (transportation, tickets and a commentary included in the price). Or you can save money by going to the ticket office at the Frontón México, Plaza de la República. Seats in the *sombra* (shade) cost more than the sunny side *(sol)*. Unless you're a bullfight veteran, you're better off in the cheaper seats higher up, farther from the explicit details of the action. Remember that this flamboyant spectacle is not a sport but a tragic ritual performance—a mystical ballet of death, both

violent and beautiful. The fanfares, costumes and protocol come from a far-off century and country. But the crowds, in and out of the *plaza de toros*, are pure Mexican, and worth savoring.

Forthcoming bullfight programs are advertised in newspapers and posters. Some of the most famous *toreros* in the world appear at Plaza México, every Sunday from around November to April (the dry season). During the rainy season, *novilladas* are often staged —bullfights for novices, with smaller bulls.

More Museums

For readers' convenience, museum hours are grouped on pp. 114–115.

City Center
Museo de la Ciudad de México, corner of Pino Suárez and República de El Salvador. In an old palace the history of Mexico City is shown in models, paintings, photographs and relics. A lighted model of present-day Mexico City gives visitors a vivid idea of the scope and size of this great metropolis. **61**

Museo de las Culturas, Moneda 13. Exhibits in this 18th-century colonial building complement the National Anthropology Museum; here the subject is the cultures of various foreign countries and Mexican tribes that are now defunct. The museum charges a small entry fee.

Museo de San Carlos, Puente de Alvarado 50. Charles III founded this art museum in the 18th century. The distinguished neo-classical building has a most original two-story oval patio. The best works on display, of the calibre you'd find in a provincial museum in Spain, are Spanish, Flemish, Dutch and Italian. Admission is free.

Pinacoteca Virreinal (Viceregal Picture Gallery), Calle Dr. Mora facing the west side of Alameda park. Colonial-era religious paintings—16th to 18th centuries—fill this comfortably refurbished old church (formerly La Iglesia de San Diego). Most of the artists are Mexican. Admission to the gallery is free.

Museo Postal, upstairs in the main post office, opposite the Fine Arts Palace. A small collection of old saddlebags, mailboxes and postal paraphernalia, just the thing for holidaying postmen.

In Chapultepec Park

Museo de Historia Natural (Natural History Museum). From baby worms to the real skeleton of a dinosaur, exhibits deal with every aspect of life on earth. This is one of Mexico's new museums, with a variety of interesting displays cleverly organized in a series of linked halls. There is a small admission charge.

Museo Tecnológico. A vast new building next to the Chapultepec amusement park. Exhibits cover modern achievements in industry, transportation and communications. Admission is free.

Insurgentes Sur

The **Polyforum Siqueiros** is a 12-sided building designed by David Alfaro Siqueiros as a big new cultural center. His most ambitious mural, a titanic three-dimensional work called *The March of Humanity*, covers the walls and ceiling of the building's circular auditorium. In fact, the auditorium was built specifically to house the 92,000 square-foot mural. Also on the premises: a theater, café, art gallery and arts-and-crafts shop. There is an admission charge for "sound-and-light" performances, as well as an entry fee to the hall containing the Siqueiros mural.

Southern Suburbs

Museo Regional de El Carmen (Carmen Museum), Avenida Revolución, San Angel. A fine old convent undergoing steeple-to-vault restoration, the better to display a collection of 17th- and 18th-century Mexican religious art. Surprising sight in the crypt: some well-dressed mummies behind glass.

An attractive shop on the premises sells faithful reproductions of pre-Hispanic sculpture. The copies, carefully produced in the museum's own workshops, make high-quality souvenirs to take back home. There is a small admission charge.

Anahuacalli, Diego Rivera Museum, Avenida del Museo, Tlalpan. This museum is astounding in three ways: the pyramidal architecture; Rivera's overwhelming private collection of pre-Hispanic sculpture and ceramics; and the atmosphere, which gives insight into the life and work of the artist. The museum was planned and constructed by Rivera as his last gift to the Mexican nation. Nearly 2,000 archaeological pieces are displayed; more than 50,000 additional items he acquired are stored nearby. In a recreated studio you can follow Rivera's career from his first drawing—a train done at age 3½—to his murals glorifying Joseph Stalin, Mao Tse-tung and the workers. Admission is free.

Museo Frida Kahlo, Allende and Londres streets, Coyoacán. Diego Rivera donated this unusual house to the nation in memory of his wife, Frida Kahlo, herself a talented painter. You'll see intimate glimpses of their life and work together. And you'll be fascinated by the brightly painted house, its enticing old tile kitchen and the archaeological relics. Admission is free.

Museo Trotsky, Viena and Morelos streets, Coyoacán. On a street where most houses hide behind high walls for privacy, this one is a literal fortress—with gun turrets, sentry boxes and high barred windows. A most melancholy place, where Leon Trotsky, Lenin's commissar of foreign affairs and war, lived in exile. All the security precautions were worthless. His shattered eyeglasses are still on the desk, the calendar turned to Tuesday, August 20, 1940, the day Trotsky was fatally axed here by an agent of Stalin. (The assassin, a Spanish communist, died in 1978 in Cuba.)

Ring the bell for entry; admission is free.

Excursions South

Cuernavaca
Pop. 300,000
85 km. (53 miles) from Mexico City

It's always springtime in this gracious year-round resort city, where the average daily temperature varies by only 9 degrees Fahrenheit from winter to summer. And after Mexico City's rarified air, the easy breathing in Cuernavaca comes as a pleasure. After all, it's *down* around 5,000 feet above sea level.

Most excursion companies run day-trips to Cuernavaca by bus or car. Or you can drive yourself: it's only an hour and a half from Mexico City via toll *(cuota)* route 95.

The cheapest outing is by bus; several leave Mexico City's Estación Tasqueña every hour. This modern bus terminal on the southern edge of the capital (convenient for the bus drivers if not for their customers) is a show in itself: country folk and their many babies heading home, and perhaps a Mexican glamour girl leading her miniature poodle aboard the air-conditioned "super-luxury" bus for Acapulco.

What to See
The **cathedral** of Cuernavaca began as a Franciscan church in the early 16th century. Three and a half centuries later it was elevated to the status of a cathedral. Then in 1957 the local bishop, a controversial avant-garde figure, decided to rip out some of the gaudy decorations accumulated over the years and refurbish the interior in modern design. The result is spectacular: a venerable cathedral decorated in blatantly up-to-date style. However, executed with simplicity and openess, it really works.

Even if you side with the conservatives who consider the renovations well-nigh blasphemous, you'll agree something marvelous did come from the project. Long lost under layers of paint and dust, murals like none other in Mexico were discovered here. The 16th-century paintings commemorate the Cuernavaca friars who went to the Far East on missionary expeditions. Twenty-six were martyred. Their trials are illustrated here in a rare dispassionate style, suggesting that the artists came from the orient — probably Japan or the Philippines.

The cathedral and two small churches occupy a roomy, rest- **65** ful enclave. Across the busy Avenida Morelos is another quiet precinct, the **Jardines Borda** (Borda Gardens). This city park (small entry fee) is more notable for its historical associations than any specific beauty or charm. The gardens were established by the 18th-century "silver king" of Taxco, José de la Borda. Emperor Maximilian and Charlotte are said to have enjoyed the tranquility that can be found here. An Olympic-sized artificial duck pond makes a popular birdbath for local pigeons and crows. Otherwise the place is deserted.

The town square, or Zócalo, of Cuernavaca is a lively relic of old-time village life. Here the townsfolk and tourists lounge on white benches, resigned to being solicited every minute or two by another salesman hawking jewelry, balloons, paintings, pies, pottery, or a song and dance.

Cuernavaca has three contiguous plazas. In the biggest, the Jardín de los Héroes (Heroes' Garden), hack photographers pose children atop wooden horses provided as props—along with toy pistols, rifles and bandoliers. The pompous arcaded palace facing the plaza on the west looks like some sort of overblown historic building. However, it dates only from 1967 and is the headquarters of the state and city governments.

A genuine landmark is the gloomy crenelated fortress known as **El Palacio de Cortés** (the Palace of Cortés). From this stronghold the chief conqueror actually ruled the town and what became the state of Morelos. Like the Indians hundreds of years before him, Cortés enjoyed living in Cuernavaca's gentle climate. The palace is now open to the public (except on Thursdays) with the name "Museum of Cuaunáhuac"—the original Indian name for the town, which the Spaniards mistook for Cuernavaca ("cow's horn"). A highlight is the **mural** by Diego Rivera covering the second floor terrace. It tells the history of Cuernavaca, emphasizing the cruelty of the Spaniards towards the vanquished Indians.

A unique contrast to the usual Mexican portrayal of the conquerors is a heroic statue of Cortés himself, said to be the only one in the nation. On the grounds of a Cuernavaca hotel, the chief colonialist—bare-

Pyramid built within a pyramid is worth the climb in Cuernavaca.

headed, bearded and looking kindly—is seated on horseback atop a 30-foot-tall ivy-cloaked pedestal.

A stroll from the center of town, across a long modern footbridge spanning a ravine, leads to Cuernavaca's new market *(mercado)*. Though unexpectedly hygienic, this immense enclosed marketplace is excitingly down-to-earth: check out the different varieties of fruit and vegetables, pastries, spices and even love potions. Within the city limits of Cuernavaca is an archaeological zone which will appeal to tourists in a hurry. A short taxi ride and a small admission fee are the only obstacles. The **pyramid of Teopanzolco** is attributed to the Tlahuican tribe of Indians who lived here nearly 1,000 years ago. You can climb to the top of the restored remains. The surprise is that you're looking down onto another pyramid, enclosed within the one visible from ground level.

This discovery was made during the revolution of 1910 when Zapata's insurgent forces set up an artillery outpost on a hill northwest of the town center. The recoil of the guns chopped into the thin topsoil, revealing that it was not a hill at all, but a pyramid.

Taxco
Pop. about 60,000
171 km. (106 miles) from Mexico City

Everybody's dream of a mountainside town, Taxco is so pretty that sooner or later tourists were bound to arrive in large numbers. But hiking through the winding cobbled streets, the visitor can still find inspiration in the ever-changing views of tile-roofed white houses, flashes of bougainvillea and jacaranda and two pink church towers set against the mountains and sky. Don't run out of film when a cargo-carrying burro shuffles in front of your camera.

Taxco (pronounced in Mexican Spanish TAHSS-co) is also a serious shopping town. About one in four local residents is an artisan of some sort. Of all the handicrafts on sale in the town's hundreds of shops the most renowned are articles of silver, which is only natural because it was silver mining that put Taxco on the map in earliest colonial days.

Many excursions from Mexico City combine visits to Cuernavaca and Taxco in a single day. The drive from Cuernavaca to Taxco takes less than two hours through real cowboy country dotted with foraging cattle in wide-open spaces.

Taxco is so attractive that vacationers come all the way from the beaches of Acapulco on day-trips, enduring nearly ten hours on a bus for the round-trip excursion.

What to See

From any part of Taxco or the surrounding mountains you can see the twin double-deck towers of **Santa Prisca Church.** These complex pink stone towers seem to belong to a full-scale cathedral, but Santa Prisca is only a parish church. It was built in the mid-18th century by José de la Borda, who may have been French or Spanish. Having struck it rich in silver, he sponsored this extravagant church.

The style is called Churrigueresque in honor of a Spanish architect, José Churriguera, who was thought to have ori-

A sight worth 10 hours on a bus: hill town of Taxco, built on silver.

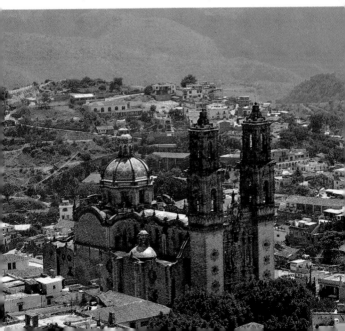

ginated this florid extension of baroque. It adds up to fantastically ornate detail on the towers, the facade and the overpoweringly lavish altars. Another feature of Santa Prisca (named after a 13-year-old girl martyred in Rome around A.D. 270) is the sacristy. There you can see highly valued religious paintings by Miguel Cabrera, a Zapotec Indian who became the leading Mexican artist of the 18th century.

Silver is closely controlled in all its stages, beginning at the local mine. More than 800 men, working round the clock, produce 2,000 tons of ore per day—yielding about 53 pounds of pure silver. Local artisans have to buy their ingots at the bank.

The residues from mining are called *jales*. The local sports stadium is called Los Jales because it was created by filling in a steep fold of the mountainside with the wastes from the mine. If a ball goes over the side it's a long way down.

The silver bonanza explains the town's modern museum, officially called El Museo de Taxco Guillermo Spratling. William Spratling was a teach-

Seen through screen of necklaces, shoppers stock up on souvenirs.

er, writer and traveler from the U.S.A. who almost accidentally detonated Taxco's 20th-century boom. Down and out and enchanted with the town, he founded a silver-smithing industry. For nearly 40 years he lived in or near Taxco, pursuing archaeology as a hobby; most of the priceless artifacts on display in the museum were Spratling's legacy to his adopted land.

A private museum is maintained in the house known as **Casa Figueroa.** This spooky palace dates from the middle of the 18th century. A local magistrate allegedly forced local Indians to build the house in lieu of paying fines; his involuntary, unpaid employees called it la Casa de las Lágrimas (the House of Tears). Presumably afraid of retribution, the judge designed it as something of a fortress. There are 26 rooms but only two windows, and both of them face interior patios. To be doubly sure, they were barred. Nonetheless, Casa Figueroa's security didn't hold up for one 20th-century resident, a rich spinster. She was murdered on the premises.

Mini-excursion

Between Taxco and Cuernavaca on sparsely traveled mountain roads, **Las Grutas de Cacahuamilpa** makes a worthwhile side trip. This unusually vast cavern—no one has explored all of it—is little-known on the main tourist beat; but it's a popular outing among the Mexicans.

If your idea of a cave is a place to escape the hot weather outside, forget it. The Cacahuamilpa cave is warm and humid. You have to walk about 2½ miles to see all the principal underground sights. Many visitors buy decorated walking sticks called *mulitas* before setting out, though they're more useful for souvenir value than for hiking.

The cave's ceiling reaches a height of more than 200 feet. Guides explain in Spanish the imaginative names given to distinctive formations of stalagmites and stalactites. They also beam a flashlight at the grave of a legendary Englishman who died exploring the cave more than a century ago. With the cement walkways and plenty of lights along the way, present-day visitors are unlikely to get lost on the tour.

The cave is open daily from 10 a.m. to 3 p.m. —to 4 p.m. on Sundays and holidays. A small entry fee is levied; children half price. Flecha Roja bus line runs a direct service from Mexico City.

Acapulco

Pop. 400,000

397 km. (247 miles) from Mexico City

This grandiose harbor—in the class of Rio and Hong Kong—is the playground of movie stars, millionaires, glamorous politicians and ordinary budget-conscious Mexicans and foreign tourists.

You don't need a private jet or yacht to enjoy Acapulco's climate, beaches, nightlife and escapism. You can hop on a bus from Mexico City; several lines operate express services from the Estación Tasqueña, and one company alone has 24

departures daily. The six-hour trip aboard a comfortable air-conditioned bus costs not much more than the taxi fare to the bus station.

From Mexico City, various firms sell organized excursions to Acapulco, often with stops in Cuernavaca and Taxco on the way.

Mexicana and Aeromexico fly from Mexico City to Acapulco in less than an hour; the fare is about four times the cost of a bus ticket.

Acapulco's outstandingly attractive airport is also served by direct flights from major U.S. and Canadian cities.

If you drive or take the bus

you'll see every kind of landscape on what is mostly a toll road. Toward the end of the grueling trip the highway winds through arid mountains brightened by occasional oases of gangly coconut palms. Then you arrive in a rundown mountain town which turns out to be a suburb of Acapulco itself. From this prosaic village you get your first startling glance down to the blue Pacific and the sweep of the famous bay.

The Port

The Spanish conquerors, who were quick to recognize a great harbour when they saw one, soon made Acapulco one of the busiest ports on the Pacific. Today the scene is even livelier. Instead of Spanish galleons unloading the spices of the orient, big white cruise liners send ashore crowds of souvenir-hungry tourists. Sightseers on excursion yachts toss coins to boys diving in the day. Water-ski boats crisscross freighters and sailboats. To the east and west of the port stretch miles of sandy beaches pounded by ocean swells or caressed by the waters of the bay.

At the center of this scene, the Zócalo is a tropical town square with plenty of benches shaded by young trees. Local chess players—and trumpet and guitar players—arrive with the evening breeze.

The main church, Acapulco's **cathedral,** is an amazing building with bulbous domes facing the Zócalo. This peculiarly Byzantine affair, which might have been built in any era, was in fact a 20th-century project.

Just down the waterfront is a more historic structure, with a floor-plan like a star, the **Fuerte de San Diego** (San Diego Fort). In the early 17th-century, British pirates began cashing in on all the treasure flowing through Acapulco—oriental exotica inbound, silver outbound. So the Spanish erected proper defenses on a small hill overlooking the port. Destroyed by an earthquake in 1776, the fortress was rebuilt in 1784.

To cross the beachside avenue, Costera Miguel Alemán, you have to dart between buses, cars, tourist jeeps, blue-and-white taxis which look alarmingly like police cars, and horse-drawn carriages (calandrias) festooned with balloons. If you're looking for an address on this main boulevard, you'll soon discover that the street-numbering system is chaotic. As a general rule, the farther east you go, the higher the numbers—but you're never quite sure!

The Beaches

For most Acapulco vacationers the top tropical topic is the beach. With such a variety to choose from, it's fashionable to use one beach in the morning and another in the afternoon to take advantage of the sun's angle and the changing tide.

The best-known morning beaches, **Caleta** and **Caletilla** (meaning "cove" and "little cove"), are lively and authentic. They can be more crowded than you'd consider comfortable, but it's all in good fun. Everyone is smiling, the tourists and the friendly locals— who also like to swim. Every couple of minutes somebody tries to sell you a straw bag, a slice of watermelon or a stuffed armadillo. No harm done.

Caleta and Caletilla are fine for children because they're protected from the open sea by a nearby island called **La Roqueta.** This is easily reached by a small ferryboat from the mainland. With an excellent

beach of its own, La Roqueta is also famous for its beer-swilling burros: these resident donkeys really are hooked on beer. Glass-bottom boats always pause on the run from Caleta to La Roqueta for a look at the underwater shrine dedicated by local fishermen, sailors and divers to the Virgin of Guadalupe.

Closer to the center of town are the yacht club, excursion boat moorings and finally the game-fishing port. Here 50 deep-sea fishing boats are available for hire by rod-and reel enthusiasts. The experts say sailfish are caught all year round, March is the best month for hooking marlin, December and January for dorado, and the summer months for shark. Underwater fishing with scuba

Looking down on the classic bay of Acapulco from cooler altitudes where fashionable homes are built.

equipment is another significant local sport.

Heading east from the Zócalo and the wharves, **Hornos Beach** is the first of the noted afternoon beaches. Like all Acapulco's beaches, it's kept admirably clean in spite of the careless habits of the populace. Teams are always at work collecting the latest rubbish, the head man raking it and his assistant assigned to deposit it in a pail.

At the afternoon beaches you'll gape at parachutists gliding over the water, towed by speedboats. This "sport" is said to have been invented in Acapulco. They'll whisk you expertly from the beach into the air and keep you aloft for as long as you can stand it. But if you weigh more than 242 pounds the deal's off; the boat's engine isn't powerful enough to launch you.

A stylish beach heading east is **La Condesa** — "the countess." The architecture of some hotels and condominiums along here is original and attractive.

The coast road, heading out of town to the east, climbs a hillside with striking views of Acapulco harbor, then reveals a bay beyond: **Puerto Marqués.** With the Acapulco skyline of hotels now invisible behind the hills, Puerto Marqués seems like an undiscovered paradise. But don't expect solitude; the beach is bustling with local families, fishermen, and the inevitable teams of souvenir, food and drink vendors. Dozens of fishermen's restaurants line this beach — primitively constructed but fun for lunch.

Down the coast beyond Puerto Marqués, **Revolcadero Beach** has such cruel surf that it's often out-of-bounds for swimming. A huge, expensive hotel on this beach compensates its guests for the problem by providing four swimming pools. The Acapulco Princess Hotel, a pyramid-shaped wonder of modern architecture and landscaping, is worth a sightseeing visit.

On the opposite side of Acapulco, **Pie de la Cuesta Beach** is about 8 miles northwest of town, on the open ocean. This is where the crowds go for an Acapulco pastime — **watching the sunset.** At Pie de la Cuesta, from the vantage point of a hammock or the sand, with drink in hand, you can consider all the romantic implications of the spectacle. As seagulls dive-bomb the fish in the dying orange light and the waves roll ashore, the Pacific sunset is truly worth savoring. In Acapulco everyone takes it seriously.

Nightlife

In 1955 the expressway linking Acapulco with Mexico City was inaugurated, unleashing the tourist rush which still booms today. For visitors requiring more excitement than the sunset and the moonlight, nightclub talent is recruited from all over the country. The floor shows run from Mexican mariachis to Spanish flamenco dancers. You can watch serious folk ballet performed in the lavish new Convention Center,

Itinerant vendor takes advantage of lowered resistance in Acapulco.

or the famous "Totonacas Flyers" *(Los Voladores)* staging an ancient, daring aerial act.

The spectacle most closely identified with Acapulco takes place half a dozen times a day, but most dramatically at night, at a cliffside called **La Quebrada.** You may have seen the high-divers *(clavadistas)* in the movies or on television, but there's no substitute for the thrill of being on the spot. From a promontory more than 130 feet above sea level, a daring young man plunges into a crevice, anticipating the exact moment when the incoming waves will flood it. The crowd reacts with a sigh and a cheer as the diver reveals himself alive and unharmed, clambering out of the surf. Dripping but triumphant, he runs up hundreds of steps through the throng of tourists, accepting congratulations and contributions. With these tips and a small admission charge to the so-called public viewing area, the 26 divers who belong to La Quebrada's closed shop make a living out of their risky endeavor. No sane tourist would consider the dive at any price.

Lonely flight: Acapulco cliff diver begins 130-foot plunge to the sea.

What to Do

Shopping

In Mexico shopping is an adventure packed with pleasure and enlightenment. Tasteful handicrafts, wildly-colored inventions and lovable peasant fashions exude all the history, tradition and talent of the people. Even the simplest and, frankly, silliest souvenirs are unmistakably Mexican. And the act of buying can be exciting in itself, more so if you let yourself be swept up in the crowds at one of the colorful outdoor markets. In tourist-oriented boutiques in the Pink Zone or near the Alameda you'll also find the prices attractive.

First, an alphabetical idea list to get you started:

Antiques. At the flea market or in luxurious shops, a fascinating range of items from brass candlesticks and old muskets to intricately carved doors from colonial churches.

Azulejos. Hand-painted tiles, in the Spanish tradition, with some indigenous touches.

Bamboo birdcages and walking-sticks.

Candelabra. The spectacular Mexican variety, earthenware, are fancifully hand-painted.

Chess sets. Ceramic or onyx.

One remarkable version has Emperor Moctezuma and his forces as the white pieces, Cortés and the conquerors as the blacks. The blacks have horses, the whites, jaguars.

Doll houses and furnishings right down to the most ingenious tiny pots and pans.

Dresses. Joyously decorated peasant styles—just the thing for summer parties—or more sophisticated versions with hand-painted Indian designs.

Embroidery. Shirts, dresses, blouses, table-linen, kerchiefs in floral designs or subtle abstract stitching.

Furniture. If shipping problems don't bother you, choose from solid Spanish-colonial chairs, onyx coffee tables or antique brass bedsteads.

Glassware. Hand-blown bowls, pitchers, glasses and figurines—often created from recycled beer bottles!

Gourds decorated in abstract designs. The musical models, *maracas*, combine color and sound (the rattling of the dried beans inside).

Guitars. From cheap souvenirs to professional instruments—a selection to suit every need.

Hats. Of straw, leather, or the glittering sombreros of the *charros* (rodeo cowboys).

Hojalatería. Tinware extravaganzas—mirror frames, candelabra, sculpture, lanterns.

Huaraches. The traditional Mexican sandals, stylish in hand-tooled leather.

Indian sculptures. Reproductions of the great archaeological discoveries—but don't scoff. They're not totally counterfeit, since the craftsmen are descendants of the original artists and often use the same materials and techniques.

Jewelry. Silver, especially: bracelets, rings, brooches, earrings in Indian and modern designs. Gold, copper and semi-precious stones are also used.

Knick-knacks. All handicraft markets overflow with nameless and often useless inventions—straw burros, ceramic frogs, miniature Aztec calendars, onyx ashtrays. But they usually look better once you get home.

Leather. Belts, handbags, jackets, luggage, shoes, wallets. In "western" style or big-city fashions.

Liquor. For warm memories of your vacation, invest in fancily-bottled tequila or coffee liqueur.

Masks. Hand-carved and -painted wooden ceremonial masks with authentic superstitious overtones.

Natural stones, right out of the ground, or polished or carved: amethyst, lapis lazuli, malachite, onyx, turquoise.

Oil paintings by Mexican artists. Familiar landscapes or portraits of country folk or modern interpretations of old indigenous themes.

Ponchos, rebozos, serapes. The clothing they still wear in the countryside in lieu of sweaters and coats, made from hand-loomed fabrics. Each region has its own patterns and colors, all unmistakably Mexican.

Pottery. No end to the imagination producing these—bowls, candlesticks, casseroles, dishes, figurines, jugs, mugs and pitchers. Infinite varieties of design and decoration.

Quixote statues. For tourists who feel Mexico is almost Spain. Carved or papier-maché.

Rugs and mats, bags and hats—of straw and similar natural fibers.

Saddles. Hand-tooled leather fit for the king of the cowboys.

Toys. Mostly simple ideas but garishly hand-decorated. *Balero*, an age-old ball-and-stick game, clay whistles in animal forms, piggy banks and *piñatas* (balloons or pots full of presents and candies) to shatter at Christmas time.

Trying to keep up with the demand for Mexican hand-painted pottery.

Vaquero (cowboy) boots. Elaborately hand-tooled. While you're there, the same stores often sell hats, spurs and whips.

"Wedding shirts" *(camisa de manta, guayabera)*. Finely embroidered men's shirt-jacket; formal enough to wear for any occasion but delightfully comfortable.

Where to Shop

For handicrafts, it really narrows down to the question: to haggle or not to haggle?

Fixed prices are the rule in chain stores, hotel gift shops, the huge Central Crafts Market facing the Buenavista railroad station and at government-run stores. These include the Museo de Industrias y Artes Populares and three government Fonart stores, all on Avenida Juárez, and all displaying the very best achievements of Mexican artisans.

But the prices are usually flexible in the many "public markets" or *tianguis* (native markets). In these situations the bargaining process is part of the experience. For tourists who can't count to 100 in Spanish, the merchants either speak a bit of English or write down offer and counter-offer on a scrap of paper. Knowledgeable buyers expect to bluff their way to a 10 to 30 per cent reduction in the asking price. It requires a sense of drama and plenty of patience. Incidentally, if you're not serious about buying, don't start haggling just for fun; this is considered bad taste.

Handmade flowers on ornamental "Tree of Life" contrast with the real thing on the way to market.

Ideally, you'll want to look at the quality and prices in the fixed-price stores and expositions before going forth to bargain. Anywhere that tourists are found you may be accosted by friendly English-speaking touts offering "information" in general or assistance with shopping. You'll do better on your own, for they make a living on the commissions they get for delivering raw tourists to certain stores.

Here's a rundown on the biggest and most popular Mexico City markets:

Ciudadela. Just north of Ciudadela Park, 300 stands arranged in an open-air setting to look like a small Mexican town. All the standard folklore items; there's also a glass-blowing operation on the premises worth watching.

Lagunilla. Exciting but only on Sundays (see p. 57).

(see p. 57).

Mercado de Londres, on Londres street between Amberes and Florencia in the Pink Zone. A curious conglomeration of handicrafts, vegetable stalls and snack-bars. Bargains may be found here, even though the market's hidden among all the pricey boutiques of this prime tourist area.

Mercado de la Merced. (Merced Metro station has an exit right in the middle of the mar-

ket.) For sight-seeing more than buying: this is the biggest market in all of Mexico, in a building that seems as big as the Pentagon. If you can take your eyes off the individually-shined tomatoes and the dozens of varieties of peppers, look at the salt-of-the-earth faces of the sales-people and customers.

San Angel. Bazaar Sábado. Only on Saturdays, the center of this southern suburb comes alive as a busy shopping area for tourists. Very attractive shops on and near the central Plaza de San Jacinto, and simpler goods sold at an open-air *tianguis* in an adjacent plaza.

San Juan handicrafts market *(mercado de curiosidades)*. Run by the city government, just northwest of Plaza del Salto del Agua. Here you'll find roomy, airy modern buildings covering a whole city block with three floors of free enterprise and independent merchants.

Mercado de Sonora. On Fray Servando Teresa de Mier, near the Sonora cinema. There's a wide variety of pottery items on sale, fascinating doll-house furniture, all kinds of miniatures and a selection of inexpensive toys. Have a look, too, at the medicinal herb department with cures for all ailments.

When to Shop

Most stores are open from 10 a.m. to 6 p.m. Monday through Friday, with extended hours till 8 p.m. on Wednesdays and Saturdays.

Warning 925

Whether you shop in a slick tourist store or amidst the hurly-burly of an open market, be alert about silver. Look for the figures "925" stamped into the metal on the back of any item purported to be silver. That's the Mexican government's guarantee that the metal is 92.5 per cent pure. Alternatively there might be a minute stamp of the national eagle-and-serpent symbol. Unless one of these tiny signs is visible on the product, no matter how vehement the salesman's re-assurances, chances are you're buying a cheap alloy called *alpaca*.

Shopping safari

Every Friday thousands of country folk converge on the small city of **Toluca,** capital of the State of Mexico, for the most colorful open market this side of Marrakesh. Tour companies run expeditions from Mexico City. Or you can take an ordinary bus—it's a bit more than an hour each way. Toluca's gigantic bus terminal is right next to the 1½-square-mile marketplace.

You may not be in the mood to buy a live baby lamb or a gawky parrot but the atmosphere of intense commerce will intrigue you. Under makeshift tents, sharp provincial merchants entice dusty Indians in cowboy hats to buy brassieres and phonograph records. In the food market, women surrounded by their children make and sell tortillas, or shout the advantages of their tomatoes, mangoes or yams. On the far side of the market, farmers carry prize pigs, turkeys or geese to be bargained over. For tourists the handicrafts section is strong on straw bags, ceramics, rough sweaters and serapes. Haggling is obligatory.

While you're in town, take the short bus or taxi ride to the center of Toluca, where you'll find a stately array of government buildings surrounding the traditional Zócalo. There are attractive colonial-style civic buildings with quiet patios, a neo-classic cathedral, a fine arts museum and a modern theater. Toluca's altitude is 8,700 feet, so don't try to see too much too fast.

Hanging around: cheerily colored Indian designs at an open tianguis.

Fiestas

No matter how solemn a festival may be, the Mexicans observe it with originality, enthusiasm and vivacity. Surrounding the genuine cause for the occasion, they add fringe benefits as irrelevant as fireworks, cockfights, rodeos, beauty-queen contests, bullfights, parades and dances.

Every town and village in the country celebrates the day of its patron saint and plenty of other local and national holidays. Any one of them will reward you with a unique mixture of Catholic and pagan manifestations, earnest devotion comfortably coexisting with hilarity.

Here are some of the most interesting fiestas:

Holy Week (March or April). To see moving demonstrations of faith go to any church, but the most astounding spectacle is Good Friday in the southeast Mexico City district of

Ixtapalapa. Local boys and men in vivid costumes recreate the way of the cross, penitents wearing crowns of real thorns and carrying heavy crosses. Tens of thousands turn out to watch, munching *tortas* and sipping coconut juice.

Corpus Christi (May or June). In mid-morning Mexico City's Zócalo is filled with mothers and children, the little girls in lavish home-made costumes and wearing lipstick, the boys in white Zapata outfits with charcoal-scrawled mustaches. While a special mass is celebrated inside the cathedral, Indian dancers—feathers and all—beat their drums outside.

All Souls' Day (November 1-2). Papier-maché skeletons and candies in the shape of skulls in this macabre celebration. Candle-light vigils at cemeteries, followed by huge feasts.

Imagination distinguishes souvenirs at fiesta and (below) hair-raising headgear worn at a folklore show.

Our Lady of Guadalupe (December 12). Many pilgrims walk all the way from their villages to the shrine, on the north side of Mexico City. Emotional displays of devotion mixed with the inevitable fun and frolics. Most notable pagan show in the great plaza: the "flying Indians" circling on ropes attached to the top of a high pole.

December 16–24. Nine days of Mexico's famous *posadas*, parties symbolizing the no-room-at-the-inn Christmas story. Fireworks and nativity plays and finally the gay *piñatas* rain down gifts so everyone can fight for the best prize.

Spectacles

Pyramids: "Luz y Sonido". An interpretation of the history of the mysterious Teotihuacán holy city in a sound-and-light show performed on the spot. Every evening except Monday from October through May. English dialogue at 7 p.m., Spanish at 8:15. Bus service from Revolution Monument at 6 p.m. Equipment failure may interrupt the program; check with the Tourism Secretariat, Masaryk 172.

Folklore Ballet. The Ballet Folklórico de México performs at the Palace of Fine Arts and at the National Auditorium on Reforma. Tickets can be bought at the box-office or at a "Boletrónico" outlet, a computerized system intended to eliminate scalpers. If you didn't love Mexico before, you surely will after the performance, ranging from eerily-recreated prehistoric Indian ceremonials to swirling petti-coats and the Mexican Hat Dance. You'll never hear better folk music in Mexico—fiddles, guitars, trumpets, drums, flutes, marimbas, a harp, and some angelic human voices. The costumes, color and choreography are excellent.

Concerts, opera. Band concerts in the park or full-dress opera in a plush theater—Mexico City's musical life is ample. Almost every night there's a worthwhile concert, perhaps by the National Symphony Orchestra or the Symphony of the State of Mexico.

Theater. If you know Spanish you can choose between a couple of dozen live plays. If you don't know Spanish, how about seeing a hit musical?

Movies. Almost all films shown in Mexico are dubbed into Spanish. However, a few theaters—usually they advertise in the English-language paper—show the original version with Spanish subtitles.

Nightlife

Mexico City doesn't claim to be one of the world's great nightlife capitals, yet you won't run out of places to go. You can move from rooftop cocktail bar to floorshow dinner club to deafening disco to intimate nightcap cellar and then start again the next night with a whole new itinerary. Most of the action centers on the big hotels and in the Pink Zone. It is believed the area won its name because in a *zona roja*

Costumes, choreography and music excel in popular folklore displays.

(red-light district) everything is tolerated, while in the *zona rosa* (pink, not red) *almost* everything goes.

A young crowd drifts to the south end of the Pink Zone, to the plaza surrounding the Insurgentes Metro station. In a brilliant city-planning stroke, what could have been a dehumanized traffic circle was turned into a center of outdoor cafés.

What could be more typical than the music of the mariachis, Mexico's strolling minstrels? It's believed "mariachi" is a corruption of the French word *mariage*; wedding celebrations have always been good business for these troubadors.

The place to see and hear the real mariachi music is Plaza Garibaldi, a corner of old colonial Spain tinged with overtones of Skid Row. Groups of musicians in snazzy, though sometimes fraying, costumes hang around this square waiting to be employed. Many engagements last only about three minutes—it depends on how many pesos change hands. Or you can have "crying trumpets" follow you to a party. Or send them to serenade a damsel, even at two in the morning. The neighbors won't mind.

90

Sports

Because of the altitude you probably won't be too anxious to engage in strenuous exercise. But if you insist, some Mexico City hotels have swimming pools, and there are a number of public pools. Tennis and golf are popular, but in the capital you'll need reciprocal privileges or an invitation from one of the private clubs. Fishing and hunting expeditions can also be arranged from Mexico City. For more information obtain *Fishing in Mexico* or *Hunting in Mexico* from your nearest Mexican National Tourist Council Office.

As for spectator sports, you can watch the familiar or the bizarre:

American football is a popular sport among Mexican universities but hasn't graduated to the professional degree.

Baseball. Another invention from north of the border, with a 16-team AAA league and charming expressions like *un hit* and *el double-play*.

Basketball. Not many Mexicans are built as tall as basketball stars ought to be, but the sport is popular on a local and international basis.

Boxing. Twice a week professional pugilists perform in Mexico City; in the lighter categories Mexicans have cut a wide international swath.

Jai-alai. The Basque ball game, fastest on earth, is played five nights a week at the Frontón México. Most of the fans are there for the betting—frantic and incomprehensible.

Racing. The season at the beautiful modern Hipódromo de las Américas, west of Chapultepec Park, runs 11 months of the year. The minimum bet is low enough for any pocket.

Soccer. As in most of the world, this brand of football is the national passion of Mexico. Aztec Stadium, scene of the World Cup in 1970, seats more than 100,000 fans.

In addition, Mexico City has busy seasons of bicycle racing, car racing, polo, tennis and wrestling.

Ride 'em, Vaquero! *Brilliant display of equestrian skill at* charro *show.*

Wining and Dining

Get set for a happy surprise: Mexican food is varied, wholesome, economical and delicious. If you think you're doomed to a diet of hot peppers and gravy-stained tortillas, you drastically underestimate one of the world's great cuisines. After all, Mexico's Indian gourmets were enjoying sumptuous banquets before the Spaniards ever arrived. The natives introduced the conquerors to some of the nicest foods anywhere: avocado, chocolate, peanuts, sweet potatoes, tomatoes and turkey.

The ingredients are still natural and fresh. Even the bread —a crisp, French-style roll— is worth a cheer.

Meal times

The Mexicans seem to be eating all the time; you can't quite tell if they're winding up a late

figs, melons, strawberries, as well as the more exotic papaya and mango.

Cheese is rather expensive. Since the Aztecs had no livestock, milk and dairy products are something of a recent innovation — only a few hundred years old. But Mexico does produce delicious ice-cream.

Beverages

Wine comes mostly from Baja California but also from the states of Querétaro and Aguascalientes. Since imported wine usually costs about four times as much as comparable Mexican wine you may want to investigate the local product. It comes white *(blanco)*, rosé and red *(tinto)*, the latter the most popular with Mexicans.

Beer from Mexico is good enough to export. Both light and dark, it's a treat for connoisseurs. The alcoholic content may attain 7 per cent.

Hard liquor made in Mexico, some of it very hard indeed, includes rum, gin and vodka. Scotch, bourbon and other imports are costly.

Tequila, the national drink, derives from the agave or century plant, not from cactus juice. It's drunk straight (with lime and salt) or in cocktails like the margarita.

98 *Kahlúa*, a coffee liqueur, is a Mexican invention in spite of the name. Other well-known liqueurs and aperitifs are bottled here under license.

Brandy from Mexican vineyards is acquiring ever more renown and popularity.

Non-alcoholic drinks

Familiar soft drinks are bottled under license in Mexico. There are also locally invented sodas with distinctive flavors.

Mineral water from the spa town of Tehuacán, Puebla, is available everywhere in small bottles.

Juices come not only in customary flavors but in rich tropical varieties.

Milk, pasteurized and homogenized, is a safe bet in good restaurants.

Tea is served either "black" (brewed from standard tea leaves) or in aromatic varieties to help cure what ails you.

Coffee, usually American-style (known as *café americano*), is very much part of the Mexican way of life. A more interesting variety is *café de olla*, cooked in an earthenware pot, with delicious hints of cinnamon, cloves and brown sugar. In sophisticated restaurants and bars frothy *cappuccino* is the favorite option to the standard white coffee, *café con leche*.

Y ROAD: Most visitors coming from the U.S. west coast prefer to take e highway to Tucson and El Paso, entering Mexico at Ciudad Juárez d continuing to Aguascalientes and Mexico City on the Pan American ute. Those coming from further east can enter from Laredo or ownsville. The road from Laredo passes Monterrey, Saltillo and San uis Potosí; from Brownsville and Matamoros you continue via Ciudad ctoria to San Luis Potosí, which is only about 120 miles (200 ometers) from the expressway into Mexico City.

The major U.S. bus lines serve Mexico at very reasonable rates. You ange buses at the border and continue in a coach owned by a Mexican ent of the original line.

When to Go

exico City's climate, called "subtropical high plateau", eliminates the sual four seasons. It is always spring-like and temperate by day. You'll ed a coat for evenings most of the year, though, as the city's altitude is lofty 7,350 feet.

The rainy season lasts from late May to early October, but this need ot be a deterrent. It almost never rains until the afternoon or evening d then only for two or three hours.

verage monthly temperatures and rainfall:

		J	F	M	A	M	J	J	A	S	O	N	D
ay	°F	66	70	75	77	79	75	73	73	73	70	68	66
	°C	19	21	24	25	26	24	23	23	23	21	20	19
ight	°F	43	43	46	52	54	55	54	54	54	50	46	43
	°C	6	6	8	11	12	13	12	12	12	10	8	6
ainfall nches)		0.2	0.3	0.4	0.5	0.2	4.2	4.9	4.1	4.6	1.3	0.6	0.3

Planning Your Budget

To give you an idea of what to expect, here's a list of average prices Mexican pesos. They must be regarded as approximate, however, inflation is running high.

Airport departure tax. National flights 20 pesos, international 100 pesos.

Airport transfer. Red Micro-bus airport–center 80 pesos per person, 125 pesos per vehicle.

Babysitters. 100–200 pesos per hour.

Buses. From Mexico City to: Acapulco 145 pesos, Taxco 55 pesos, Veracruz 150 pesos.

Car rental. *VW Sedan* 340 pesos per day, 2,390 pesos per week plus 2.2 pesos per km. *VW Brazilia/Caribe* 405 pesos per day, 2,840 pesos per week plus 2.85 pesos per km. *Dodge Dart* 535 pesos per day, 3,730 pesos per week plus 3.00 pesos per km. Add 10% sales tax. Collision coverage 160 pesos per day.

Cigarettes. 15.50 pesos per packet of 20, Mexican pipe tobacco 50 pesos.

Entertainment. *Nightclub* from 170 pesos admission to 1,500 pesos including dinner. *Discotheque* 170–200 pesos entry fee. *Cinema* 25–2 pesos.

Guides. 1,100 pesos a day with car in town (1,500 pesos outside) 80 pesos a day without car, 600 pesos for half day with car, 450 pesos for half day without car.

Hairdressers. *Man's* haircut 125–300 pesos. *Woman's* haircut 200–500 pesos, wash and set 200–300 pesos, color rinse 300–600 pesos.

Hotels (double room with bath). *AA* 1,250 pesos and up, *A* 600–1,00 pesos, *B* 400–600 pesos, *C* 200–330 pesos, *D* 80–180 pesos. Add 10% sales tax. These are Mexico City rates. Prices in Acapulco will be around 20% higher.

Meals and drinks. *Breakfast* 80–120 pesos, lunch/dinner in fairly good establishment 220–500 pesos, *coffee* 15–20 pesos, *beer/soft* drink 15–3 pesos, *gin and tonic* 60–80 pesos, *margarita cocktail* 60–80 pesos, *whiske* 60–80 pesos.

Taxi (standard). Zócalo–Plaza de Toros 60 pesos, Alameda–Chapultepec 40 pesos, Tlatelolco–Zona Rosa 40 pesos, Zona–Airport 150 pesos.

BLUEPRINT for a Perfect Trip

An A-Z Summary of Practical Information and Facts

Contents

A star (*) following an entry indicates that relevant prices are to be found on page 102.

Listed after some entries is the appropriate Spanish translation, usually in the singular, plus a number of phrases that may come in handy during your stay in Mexico.

Although every effort has been made to ensure the accuracy of the information contained in this book, changes will inevitably occur, and we would be pleased to hear from readers of any new developments.

A **ACCOMMODATIONS*** *(alojamiento)*. See also CAMPING. Mexican **hotel** prices are controlled by the government and cover a spectacular range from extremely cheap to painfully expensive. Budget-conscious visitors who don't require the most lavish facilities can find many clean, simple hotels at attractive prices.

The Mexican Secretary of Tourism Office classes hotels in the following manner: AA, A, B, C and D (from Super de-luxe (AA) to de-luxe, standard and so on). 10% IVA (VAT or sales tax) is added to all hotel bills.

Other accommodations include **furnished apartments** *(amueblados* or *suites)* which provide the opportunity to set up housekeeping. Hotel services are often included in the price, which is below comparable hotel rates. Look for ads in the morning newspapers. Several **motels** have been opened within easy driving distance of the downtown area.

In Acapulco and other coastal resorts hotel rates suffer significant increases during the winter season — from mid-December to the end of the Easter holidays.

Youth hostels *(albergue de juventud)* operate in the Mexico City area, though there are none in the city center. For details, inquire at the Secretariat of Tourism (see TOURIST INFORMATION OFFICES), or at CREA *(Consejo Nacional de Recursos para la Atención de la Juventud)*:

Serapio Rendón 76; tel. 591-01-44, ext. 118

Otherwise, very cheap accommodations may be found at simple *casas de huéspedes* (guest houses).

I'd like a single/double room.	**Quisiera una habitación sencilla/doble.**
with bath/shower	**con baño/ducha**
What's the rate per night?	**¿Cuál es el precio por noche?**

AIRPORT* *(aeropuerto)*. Benito Juárez International Airport is so close to town that it's actually inside the city limits. Arriving passengers receive quick, cordial clearance through immigration and customs formalities.

In the international arrivals section one team of porters carries bags to the frontier of the customs zone, where another relay takes over for the walk to the bus stop.

Micro-buses take passengers to hotels in the central area. If you have no hotel reservations there are accommodation desks and phones inside the air terminal.

Other facilities include a duty-free shop, gift and souvenir shops, banks, bars, restaurants, news-stands, post office, pharmacy and a long-distance telephone service.

A small airport tax is levied on both national and international flights.

Porter!	**¡Mozo!**
Taxi!	**¡Taxi!**
Where's the bus for...	**¿Dónde está el camión para...?**

BABYSITTERS* *(niñera)*. Hotels can usually organize baby-sitting services for their guests. Rates depend on the hotel, day of the week and number of children.

Can you get me a babysitter for tonight?	**¿Puede conseguirme una niñera para esta noche?**

CAMPING. There are two camping sites in Mexico City and several more in surrounding areas. You can have details on regulations in the brochure *Camping in Mexico* from the Mexican National Tourist Council:

Mariano Escobedo 726, México 5, D.F.

or get information from:

Deportes Camper, Avenida Universidad 700, México 13, D.F.

May we camp here?	**¿Podemos acampar aquí?**
We have a tent/trailer.	**Tenemos una tienda de camping/ una caravana.**

CAR RENTAL* *(carros de alquiler)*. International and local car rental firms have offices throughout Mexico City. A wide variety of cars are available. The rates given on page 102 are sample prices for Mexico City (the tariffs are higher in coastal resorts).

C

General conditions: You must be at least 25 years old with a valid driver license. You may have to pay a deposit unless you settle your bill b credit card. Sales tax is extra, but liability and third-party insurance included in the rates.

I'd like to rent a car for today/ tomorrow.	**Quisiera rentar un carro para hoy/mañana.**
for one day/a week	**por un día/una semana**

CIGARETTES, CIGARS, TOBACCO* *(cigarrillos, puros, tabaco,* All cigarettes, cigars and tobacco products legally on sale are manufac tured in Mexico. Several famous American brands are made local under license; others are encountered as contraband.

A pack of ..., please.	**Una cajetilla de ..., por favor.**
filter-tipped	**con filtro**
without filter	**sin filtro**
A box of matches, please.	**Una caja de cerillos, por favor.**

CLOTHING. You'll never need an overcoat in Mexico City but you' be glad you brought a raincoat between May and October. Be prepare for wide variations in temperature every 24 hours. Though you'r dressed for summer at midday you'll probably need a sweater at dusk

As in any sophisticated city in the evening, men wear a jacket and ti and women often wear long dresses in the better restaurants an nightclubs. In the daytime, however, informality is the rule. Do you sight-seeing in total comfort. But Mexico City is not a seaside resor common sense is required. For instance, shorts are inappropriate on cit streets, and if you're visiting historic churches remember that modesty expected.

Will I need a jacket and tie?	**¿Necesito saco y corbata?**

COMMUNICATIONS

Post offices *(correos)*. Mexico City's central post office is housed in Victorian palace at San Juan de Letrán and Tacuba streets.

Hours

Central post office: 7 a.m. to midnight Monday through Friday, ti 8 p.m. on Saturdays, till 4 p.m. on Sundays.

General delivery: 9 a.m. to 8 p.m. Monday through Friday, till 5 p.m on Saturdays.

Branch post offices: 9 a.m. to 7 p.m. Monday through Friday, 9 a.m. to 1 p.m. on Saturdays.

Mailboxes are marked "SCT" *(Secretaría de Comunicaciones y Transportes).* If you see three mailboxes in a row, they're designated *Aéreo* (airmail only), *D.F.* (local mail only) and *Terrestre* (surface mail). Always use airmail for foreign destinations.

General delivery (poste restante). If you don't know in advance where you'll be staying in Mexico City, you can have your mail addressed c/o *Lista de Correos* to Window 6 on the main floor of the central post office (see above), where the sign says *Lista y Poste Restante.* Take your passport or other identification when you go to pick up mail.

Telegrams *(telegrama).* The main international telegraph office is at Balderas 15 (near the west end of Alameda Park). It's open from 8 a.m. to midnight daily for cable and telex services.

Telephone *(teléfono).* The Mexico City telephone system has many critics, but it is far more efficient than the service in the provinces.

You can telephone from a café or shop as well as from a booth.

Your hotel operator can handle long-distance and overseas calls. Or you can go to one of the operator-attended long-distance offices around Mexico City. A full page of addresses appears under "Casetas de Larga Distancia" at the beginning of the white pages of the telephone directory.

Can you get me this number in...?	**¿Puede comunicarme a este número en...?**
collect (reversed-charge) call	**por cobrar**
person-to-person (personal) call	**persona a persona**
I want to send a telegram to...	**Quisiera mandar un telegrama a...**
Have you received any mail for...?	**¿Ha recibido correo para...?**
A stamp for this letter/postcard, please.	**Por favor, un sello para esta carta/tarjeta.**
special delivery (express)	**urgente**
airmail	**correo aéreo**
registered	**registrado**

COMPLAINTS *(reclamación).* If you have a complaint against a hotel, restaurant, taxi driver or tourist guide, and you can't work it out face to face, go to the Tourism Office (see below). In this office you'll find the Dirección General de Supervisión, which deals with such problems. **107**

C

For grievances involving people or organizations not normally associated with the tourism industry it's recommended that you go to the local police station.

Secretaría de Turismo, Avenida Presidente Masaryk 172, México 5, D.F.

CONVERTER CHARTS. For fluid and distance measures, see page 111. Mexico uses the metric system.

Temperature

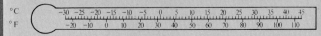

Length

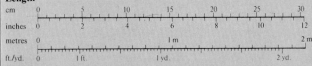

Weight

grams	0	100	200	300	400	500	600	700	800	900	1 kg
ounces	0		4	8	12	1 lb.	20	24	28	2 lb.	

COURTESIES. Dignity and politeness characterize most Mexican people. You'll be expected to do more handshaking than is your custom at home, and "please" *(por favor)* or "thank you" *(gracias)* are said at every turn. The handshaking ritual is vital on meeting and taking leave of anyone, even if the interval is only a matter of seconds. An "escalated" handshake is the *abrazo*, a bear-hug, connoting warm friendship or a special occasion (see also MEETING PEOPLE).

If you have any business meetings in Mexico be warned that they have to begin with small-talk about families or the weather; to plunge into business at the outset is considered bad form.

In a restaurant you will almost never be given the bill until you ask for it, no matter how long you wait.

How are you?   ¿Cómo está usted?

CUSTOMS *(aduana)* **and ENTRY REGULATIONS.** To enter Mexico you need a tourist card, valid from three to six months. U.S. and Canadian citizens may obtain this card at no cost, either at any Mexican onsulate or at border points. International airline companies which erve Mexico issue them routinely before flight time. To get this card you ave to show a valid passport, birth certificate or other proof of itizenship. Nationals of other countries should consult an airline ompany or Mexican consulate in their country for tourist card equirements.

You must present your tourist card when you *leave* Mexico. And any ourist who loses his card while in Mexico may have to wait hours as fficials won't let you go until they've looked up their duplicate records.

For almost all visitors from the U.S. and Canada the customs and nmigration checks at Mexico City's Benito Juárez airport are over efore you realize they're happening.

Baggage inspection has been eliminated for foreign tourists arriving in Mexico City on international flights, except in very rare cases. Tourists rriving in Mexico by car undergo a baggage check at the border.

The law permits tourists to bring a reasonable quantity of personal elongings with them including camera and up to 20 rolls of film. Movie-camera film must be restricted to 8-mm or super-8 unless you ave special permission.

The following chart shows what main duty-free items you may take nto Mexico and, when returning home, to your own country:

Into:	Cigarettes		Cigars		Tobacco	Spirits	Wine
Mexico	400	or	50	and	1 kg.	2 bottles total	
Canada	200	and	50	and	900 gr.	1.1 l. total	
U.K. and Eire	200	or	50	or	250 g	1 l. and 2 l. or 0 l. and 4 l.	
U.S.A.	200	and	100	and	*	1 l. total	

* a reasonable quantity.

Returning U.S. residents have a $300 exemption from U.S. import duty. Canadians get a $150 exemption.

have nothing to declare.   **No tengo nada que declarar.**
t's for my personal use.   **Es para mi uso personal.**

D DRIVING IN MEXICO

Entering Mexico. Customs officials issue an automobile entry permit a the border when you present your car registration certificate. If anyon other than the owner of the car is planning to drive it while in Mexico, b sure to make arrangements at the customs. Of course, all drivers requir valid licenses.

Insurance is not obligatory in Mexico, but any prudent driver wi want a short-term liability policy like those sold at the border. Norma U.S. policies do not cover accidents in Mexico. It's wise to have your ca thoroughly checked out before you leave home, in view of the scarcity c service stations and spare parts on the highways.

Driving conditions. Main roads are adequate though they tend to b narrower than comparable highways north of the Rio Grande. Th speed limit is 100 kilometers per hour (kph, or 62 mph) on the open roa unless otherwise posted. In towns, however, speed is limited to 40 kp (about 25 mph). Be extra careful in villages lest you suddenly come upo people or livestock in the road.

Do not drive cross-country at night. If you must, note this peculiarity at a narrow bridge or one-lane portion of road, the car which blinks it lights first is seizing the right of way, not yielding, as in some countries

Whenever your fuel tank reaches the halfway mark it's time to fill up gas stations are far apart.

If you are involved in an accident, or witness one, never move a injured person. According to Mexican law you must wait for a ambulance.

Driving in Mexico City. Courtesy is all but forgotten when city driver get behind the wheel. It's everyone for himself; yielding the right of wa is virtually unheard of. For drivers from countries with more discipline traffic, the best bet is to use public transportation within the capital; i saves gray hairs and tempers. If you do drive in Mexico City or othe high-altitude cities remember the thin air can affect you in curious ways For this reason, among others, never drink and drive.

In an attempt to unstop some of the worst bottlenecks in Mexic City's traffic, an extensive network of cross-city boulevards *(ejes viales* are being inaugurated. These come equipped with their own distinctiv traffic lights, signs and traffic police, and, on the one-way streets, th unusual and sometimes alarming feature of having the buses comin *against* the traffic flow. The bus lane is set apart by red markers. Driver should be extremely cautious when venturing on to these boulevards fo the first time.

Parking. The center of Mexico City is well supplied with parking meters. Parking lot attendants operate in other busy zones. These car-watchers wear uniforms similar to the police. As you leave, give the person a few pesos when he directs you into the traffic. Downtown you'll find multi-story garages.

Traffic police. In Mexico the traffic police are generally lenient with foreign tourists except in cases of grave infractions. On-the-spot fines are often delivered for being caught over-parking, blocking traffic for lack of fuel and speeding or driving on the sidewalk.

The traffic police are widely accused of soliciting bribes *(mordidas)*. Tourists would do well never to offer bribes. You can threaten to complain to the authorities.

Fuel and oil. Pemex, the government fuel company, runs all the gasoline stations. Two classes of gasoline are sold: *Nova* (81 octane) and *Extra* (92 octane) as well as lubricating oil of various companies. Foreign credit cards are not accepted at filling stations.

You should tip the attendant a few pesos for filling the tank or several pesos if other services are required.

Fluid measures

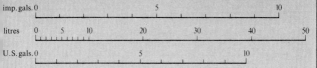

Distance

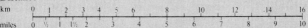

Breakdowns. The Mexican Government Secretary of Tourism runs an admirable free service for emergency assistance which can handle, on the spot, the most frequently encountered car problems. The "green angels", as these patrols are called, cover all main tourist roads. The patrolmen are bilingual and expert in car repairs and first aid.

For more serious repairs go to a garage affiliated with one of the major auto manufacturers. Look in the yellow pages of the telephone book under "Automóviles — Agencias y Compra-Venta".

Road signs. Most Mexican road signs are the standard international pictographs. But you may encounter these written signs:

111

D

Aduana	Customs
¡Alto!	Stop!
Autopista (de peaje)	(Toll) highway
Camino deteriorado	Bad road
Ceda el paso	Yield
Cruce peligroso	Dangerous intersection
Cuidado	Caution
Despacio	Slow
Desviación	Detour
Escuela	School
¡Peligro!	Danger!
Prohibido estacionarse	No parking
Prohibido rebasar	No passing
Puesto de socorro	First-aid station
Salida de camiones	Truck exit

(international) driver's license	**licencia para manejar (internacional)**
car registration papers	**registro del automóvil**
Are we on the right road for...?	**¿Es ésta la carretera hacia...?**
Fill the tank, please, top grade.	**Llénelo, por favor, con super.**
Check the oil/tires/battery, please.	**Por favor, revise el aceite/ las llantas/la batería.**
I've had a breakdown.	**Mi carro se ha descompuesto.**
There's been an accident.	**Ha habido un accidente.**

DRUGS. While the Mexican government has eased its stern campaign somewhat, anyone apprehended with significant quantities of drugs is still in for a very bad time: for a starter, one year in jail without trial.

E

ELECTRIC CURRENT *(corriente eléctrica)*. Mexico City is on 125-Volt, 60-cycle current.

EMBASSIES *(embajada)*

Canada. Melchor Ocampo 463, tel. 533-06-10

Eire. Av. Chapultepec 18, 2nd floor, tel. 510-38-67

Great Britain. Lerma 71, tel. 511-48-80

U.S.A. Paseo de la Reforma 305, tel. 553-33-33

Where's the... embassy?	**¿Dónde está la embajada...?**
American/British/Canadian/ Irish	**americana/británica/canadiense/ irlandesa**

112

EMERGENCIES *(urgencia)*. If your hotel receptionist isn't handy to help and you have a real crisis, here are some telephone numbers:

Cruz Verde (ambulance) and Emergency Radio Patrol	06
Police	588-51-00
Fire	768-37-00
Tourist highway patrol	250-46-37/53

GUIDES* *(guía)*. All official tourist guides have credentials issued by the Mexican Government Secretary of Tourism. Some guides provide and drive cars.

We'd like an English-speaking guide.	**Queremos un guía que hable inglés.**
I need an English interpreter.	**Necesito un intérprete de inglés.**

HAGGLING. In most of the big handicrafts markets, bargaining over the price is part of the excitement. If the dramatics make you uncomfortable, simply ask whether there's a discount. This may well disarm the salesperson by 10%. For some people the haggling spoils the shopping pleasure, especially if they aren't used to it. They should stick to the fixed-price establishments, such as the Museo de Industrias y Artes Populares (see p. 82). Of course department stores and other major establishments post their prices. which are not subject to negotiation.

Is there a discount?	**¿Me hace una rebaja?**

HAIRDRESSERS*. The rates on page 102 are sample prices from tourist hotel hairdressers. Neighborhood barber shops *(peluquería)* and hairdressers *(salón de belleza)* charge considerably less.

For tipping suggestions, see TIPPING.

No too much off (here).	**No corte mucho (aquí).**
A little more off (here).	**Un poco más (aquí).**
haircut	**corte**
wash and set	**lavado y peinado**
permanent wave	**permanente**
color rinse	**reflejos**

HEALTH and MEDICAL CARE. See also EMERGENCIES. Take it easy until you're accustomed to the high altitude, which may strain your heart and lungs; the smog doesn't help matters either. Drink with moderation.Eat carefully, too, for your digestion works more slowly

H

than at sea level. As for the threat of the *turistas,* a debilitating stomac episode (also known here as "Montezuma's revenge") choose your foo and drink with great care. To be on the safe side don't patronize thos street stands selling tempting snacks and fruit drinks. If the wor happens, any pharmacy will know what to do for you.

To be at ease, make sure your health insurance policy covers an illness or accident while on holiday. If not, ask your insuranc representative, automobile association or travel agent for details o special travel insurance.

Your hotel or embassy would provide a list of recommended doctor Major hospitals recognize standard medical insurance policies, but yc may have to pay cash and then ask for reimbursement upon retur home.

Farmacias (drugstores or pharmacies) are normally open durin shopping hours only. However, a number of major drugstores opera 24-hour service, seven days a week. Hotel receptionists or taxi drive have their addresses.

I need a doctor/dentist.	**Necesito un médico/dentista.**
I've a pain here.	**Me duele aquí.**
a fever	**fiebre**
sunburn	**quemadura del sol**
a stomach ache	**molestias de estómago**

HOURS. See also under COMMUNICATIONS and MONEY MATTERS. Th siesta is on the way out in modern Mexico City. All major stores an offices work straight through the lunch hour. Civil servants don't tak more than two hours for lunch. Institutions in the province, howeve tend to close from 2 to 4 p.m. at least.

Considering the high altitude, newly-arrived tourists are advised support the old tradition and take a siesta to prepare for the la afternoon and evening activities.

Castillo de Chapultepec (castle) is open from 9 a.m. to 5:40 p.m. dail **Polyform Siqueiros** (cultural center) is open 10 a.m. through 9 p.m. dail

Museums

Anahuacal.li (Diego Rivera Museum, Tlalpan). 10 a.m. – 6 p.m. dai except Monday.

Galería de Historia. 9 a.m. – 5 p.m. Tuesday through Saturday, 10 a.m. 4 p.m. on Sundays, closed Monday.

114 **Museo de Arte Moderno.** 11 a.m. – 7 p.m. daily except Monday.

Museo de la Ciudad de Mexico. 9:30 a.m. – 7:30 p.m. daily except Monday.

Museo de las Culturas. 9:30 a.m. – 6 p.m. daily except Sunday.

Museo Frida Kahlo (Coyocán). 10 a.m. – 5 p.m. daily except Monday.

Museo de Historia Natural. 10 a.m. – 5 p.m. Tuesday through Saturday, till 6 p.m. on Sundays, closed Monday.

Museo Nacional de Antropología. 9 a.m. – 7 p.m. daily except Monday.

Museo de San Carlos. 10 a.m. – 5 p.m. daily except Monday.

Museo Tecnológico. 9 a.m. – 5 p.m. Tuesday through Saturday, till 2 p.m. on Sundays, closed Monday.

Museo Trotsky (Coyocán). 10 a.m. – 5 p.m. daily except Monday.

El Palacio de Cortés (Museum of Cuaunáhuac, Cuernavaca). 10:30 a.m. – 6 p.m. daily except Thursday.

Pinacoteca Virreinal (picture gallery). 10 a.m. – 5 p.m. daily except Monday.

LANGUAGE. After Chinese and English, the most widely spoken language in the world is Spanish – from Madrid to Mexico to Manila. The Mexican variety is sweet and clear and differs slightly from that of Spain, much as American English does from English spoken in Great Britain. There are certain differences in expression, too. Around the countryside 58 indigenous languages are spoken, but Spanish is the official and universal tongue. Mexicans appreciate it if you try out your high school Spanish, however rusty it may be.

English is understood in hotels and tourist-oriented establishments throughout the country.

Good morning/Good day	**Buenos días**
Good afternoon/Good evening	**Buenas tardes**
Good night	**Buenas noches**
Thank you	**Gracias**
You're welcome	**De nada**
Please	**Por favor**
Goodbye	**Adiós**

The Berlitz phrase book, LATIN-AMERICAN SPANISH FOR TRAVELLERS, covers most situations you are likely to encounter in your visit to Mexico; also useful is the Berlitz Spanish-English/English-Spanish pocket dictionary, containing a special menu-reader supplement. See also page 125 for SOME USEFUL EXPRESSIONS.

L

LOST PROPERTY *(objetos perdidos)*. First check at your hotel reception desk, then notify the nearest police station or the Tourism Assistance (tel. 250-01-23) for lost property.

Lost children. Normally a lost child would be delivered to the neighborhood police station, which is where you should go if you lose a child – or find one. You can also telephone "Locatel" (658-11-11), a computerized information service, which will research the whereabouts of lost children.

I've lost my wallet/handbag/ **He perdido mi cartera/bolso/**
passport. **pasaporte.**

MAPS. A road map of Mexico, including a detailed plan of tourist areas of Mexico City, is issued free at the Mexican Secretariat of Tourism (see Tourist Information Offices). Car-rental firms usually provide maps for their customers. Many city and national maps are sold at newsstands and bookstores.

a street plan of... **un plano de la ciudad de...**
a road map of this region **un mapa de carreteras de esta zona**

M

MEETING PEOPLE. Traditional Spanish-style chaperones are rarely seen here anymore, but Mexico's "swinging youth" live a more controlled life than their peers in the U.S. or Canada. Unmarried girls in particular follow a strict moral code which might disappoint visiting bachelors. It is best to avoid the *abrazo,* or friendly hug, in the case of feminine friends unless the girl extends her arms first. And don't be surprised if big brother comes along on a date.

On the other side of the coin, North American women who are no longer used to exaggerated jealousy or double standards may find the "macho" attitude of Mexican men very restrictive. See also Courtesies.

MONEY MATTERS

Currency *(moneda)*. The monetary unit of Mexico is the *peso,* often abbreviated "m.n." *(moneda nacional)* or "$". The peso is divided into 100 *centavos.*

Coins: 10, 20 and 50 centavos and 1, 5, 10, 20 and 100 pesos, the latter a collector's item of silver.

Bills: 10 (rare), 20, 50, 100, 500, 1,000, 5,000 and 10,000 pesos.

There is no limit to the amount of currency you can take in or out of

Banks and currency-exchange offices *(banco; cambio)*. Most banks are open from 9 a.m. to 1:30 p.m., Monday through Friday. American Express operates 9 a.m. to 2 p.m. and 4 to 6 p.m. Monday through Friday and Saturday from 9 a.m. to 1 p.m.

The bank branches at the airport are open 24 hours a day. You may also change money—usually at slightly disadvantageous rates—in most hotels.

Credit cards and traveler's checks *(tarjeta de crédito; cheque de viajero)*. Internationally known credit cards are widely accepted in hotels, restaurants and tourist-related businesses in Mexico City. Off the main tourist routes, however, all transactions are in pesos.

Many hotels, travel agencies, shops and restaurants accept traveler's checks, but it's wiser to cash them at a bank for the best exchange rate. Take your passport or tourist card along for identification when cashing traveler's checks.

Prices. As in other countries, tourist restaurants charge vastly more than comparable establishments aiming at the local market. If you can read a menu in Spanish, why not try the menu of the day *(comida corrida)* for perhaps one-third the price of the same meal *à la carte*. Note that 10% tax and 15% service charge are added to the bill.

The prices on page 102 are representative of what the tourist is likely to meet in Mexico City; they may be even higher in coastal resorts like Acapulco, and don't forget that inflation is ever prevalent.

I want to change some dollars/pounds.	**Quiero cambiar dólares/libras.**
Do you accept traveler's checks?	**¿Acepta usted cheques de viajero?**
Can I pay with this credit card?	**¿Puedo pagar con esta tarjeta de crédito?**
How much?	**¿Cuánto es?**
Have you anything cheaper?	**¿Tiene algo más barato?**

NEWSPAPERS and MAGAZINES *(periódico; revista)*. About 30 newspapers and almost 250 magazines are published in Mexico City, so if you can read Spanish you'll easily keep up with the news. An English-language daily, *The News,* appears seven days a week with coverage aimed at the foreign "colony". Major U.S. newspapers are received by air every day and sold at principal news-stands and bookstores, which also carry leading American magazines. Some British and other

European publications may also be found, usually several days afte publication.

Have you any English-language newspapers/magazines?	**¿Tiene periódicos/revistas en inglés?**

PETS and VETS. If you want to bring your pet to Mexico you'll have t produce a rabies vaccination certificate and a veterinary health certifi cate at the border. Veterinarians are in good supply in Mexico City you'll find them listed under "Médicos Veterinarios Zootecnistas" in th telephone directory's yellow pages.

PHOTOGRAPHY. Well-known brands of film are widely available i all varieties. Processing takes about five days but many prefer to take th film home for development.

One photographic problem you may never have expected: tim exposures of night scenes in central Mexico City never work. Because c the soft terrain, every time a bus or truck goes past your tripod, the eart moves and the picture blurs.

I'd like a film for this camera, please.	**Quisiera un rollo para esta cámara por favor.**
a film for color pictures	**un rollo en color**
a black-and-white film	**un rollo en blanco y negro**
a color-slide film	**un rollo de transparencias**
35-mm-film	**un rollo de treinta y cinco**
super-8	**super ocho**
How long will it take to develop (and print) this film?	**¿Cuánto tardará en revelar (y sacar copias de) este rollo?**
May I take a picture?	**¿Puedo tomar una foto?**

POLICE *(policía)*. Mexico City's police is divided into two separat branches—the traffic and criminal divisions. All policemen and po licewomen are friendly and helpful to foreign tourists. About 35 of them designated as linguists, wear rectangular badges showing the flags of th countries whose languages they speak fluently. These special touris police are stationed in the Pink Zone and similar areas where visitor congregate.

Where's the nearest police station?	**¿Dónde está la delegación de policía más cercana?**

PUBLIC HOLIDAYS *(día festivo)*. The Mexican *fiesta* calendar offers an ample number of celebrations (almost 30), but on only 10 are shops and museums closed.

January 1	*Año Nuevo*	New Year's Day
February 5	*Aniversario de la Constitución*	Constitution Day
March 21	*Nacimiento de Benito Juárez*	Birthday of Benito Juarez
May 1	*Día del Trabajo*	Labor Day
May 5	*Batalla de Puebla*	Day of the Battle of Puebla (1862)
September 1	*Informe presidencial*	President's report, first day of Congress
September 16	*Día de la Independencia*	Independence Day
October 12	*Día de la Raza*	Columbus Day, "Day of the Race"
November 20	*Aniversario de la Revolución*	Anniversary of the Mexican Revolution
December 25	*Navidad*	Christmas Day
Movable dates:	*Pascua*	Easter: Thursday afternoon, Good Friday, Saturday and Easter Sunday

Are you open tomorrow?   **¿Está abierto mañana?**

PUBLIC TRANSPORTATION. Mexico City's cheap and well-organized public transportation system operates from 6 a.m. to about midnight.

Metro. The subway (underground) system consists of five connecting lines covering a large area of the capital. It's a fast, quiet, cheerful and inexpensive mode of transportation. Each station is identified by its own hieroglyph (an aid to rushed commuters, the near-sighted and illiterate) and marked by the sign "M" for Metro. Some routes aren't covered by the Metro (Reforma, for example) and are serviced only by bus or taxi.

Buses*. Millions of passengers use the buses every day in Mexico City, and at certain hours most of them seem to be squeezed into the very bus you're on. Don't travel during the peak hours in any case, and to escape **119**

P the crowds take the *Delfin* (dolphin) buses with 45 seats and no standees allowed.

Although there is no national bus line, there are numerous privately owned ones which operate outside of Mexico City to many otherwise inaccessible places. There are several classes, but it's recommended to take super de-luxe, de-luxe or first class for long-distance travel. All seats on these buses must be reserved.

Taking a normal inter-city bus for long-distance excursions, rather than a scheduled organized tour, will undoubtedly come out cheaper.

Some approximate times of travel: Mexico City to Taxco 4 hours, to Acapulco 6 hours, to Veracruz 8 hours.

A central bus-ticket agency *(Central de Autobuses)* in Mexico City supplies information, makes reservations and sells tickets. It's located at Reforma 52–53.

Peseros (colectivos). These jitney cabs pack six passengers into a taxi for travel along predetermined routes. The route is indicated by a number on the outside of the cab. When there are seats available the driver indicates how many by extending his fingers with his hand raised out the window.

Trains. Mexico City's modern Buenavista railroad station is on Insurgentes Norte about half a mile north of the center of town. Information on all Mexican train lines may be obtained in the arcade of the station, at the Oficina de Promoción y Pasajes de la Secretaría de Comunicaciones y Transportes.

When's the best bus/train to...?	**¿Cuál es el mejor autobús/tren para...?**
I'd like to make seat reservations.	**Quiero reservar asientos.**
one-way (single)	**ida**
round-trip (return)	**ida y vuelta**
first/second/third class	**primera/segunda/tercera clase**

R **RADIO and TV** *(radio; televisión).* Six television channels and over 50 radio stations fill the Mexico City airwaves. One local radio station, XEVIP (1560 kc.), carries CBS news programs in English usually every hour.

Late at night U.S. and Canadian stations may be picked up on medium-wave receivers. On short-wave you can hear Voice of America, BBC and Radio Canada International.

Three channels have been approved by the Mexican ministry for **citizen's band radio;** one is for communication between individual ourists, a second for intercommunication among recreational vehicles raveling as a caravan, and a third for contacting the tourist highway assistance patrol who can also provide tourist information.

RELIGIOUS SERVICES *(servicio religioso)*. The predominant religion in Mexico is Roman Catholic, but other denominations are also represented. Services in English are held in several Protestant and Catholic churches. Jewish services are in Hebrew and Spanish, but English is sometimes added. Details of all religious services are published every Friday in the local English-language daily, *The News*.

What time is mass/the service?   **¿A qué hora es la misa/el culto?**

Is it in English?   **¿Es en inglés?**

TAXIS★ *(taxi)*. Plentiful and inexpensive, Mexico City's taxis come in a variety of sizes, colors and prices. Full-sized cabs charge more than mini-taxis which are yellow VWs with room for two or three passengers. Fare is calculated according to both time and mileage. Meters don't always seem to work, so ask what the approximate fare will be before getting out. This is also true outside of Mexico City where the fare is often paid before boarding a cab to avoid later problems over the charge. Extra charge is made for baggage, etc., and is in accordance with an official sticker on the side window. After 10 p.m. a 10% surcharge is added. Fare to the airport is about double the figure on the meter. Taxis available at tourist-hotel cab stands are extremely expensive and their fares are subject to negotiation.

Flag down taxis from the curb by waving, but don't whistle. Whistling down anyone is considered the height of bad manners. For information on jitney cabs, the green and white *peseros,* see PUBLIC TRANSPORTATION. Tipping is not customary, but is appreciated by the capital's 70,000 taxi drivers.

What's the fare to...?   **¿Cuánto es la tarifa a...?**

THEFT. Wherever crowds are dense—in buses, the Metro and the flea market—pickpockets are a real menace. Be alert.

Always lock your car, even if you're only away for a few minutes, and *never* leave bags or property visible in the car, even when locked. Don't leave your baggage or packages unattended at the airport or outside a hotel.

I want to report a theft.   **Quiero denunciar un robo.**

T **TIME DIFFERENCE.** Mexico City is on Central Standard Time year round.

Time chart (winter)					
Los Angeles	Chicago	**Mexico City**	New York	London	Paris
10 a.m.	noon	**noon**	1 p.m.	6 p.m.	7 p.m.

What time is it?   **¿Qué hora es?**

TIPPING. Since a service charge is not included in hotels and restaurant bills, it's appropriate to tip waiters, porters, bellboys etc. for their efforts. Follow the chart below for rough guidelines.

Hotel porter, per bag	10 pesos
Bellboy, errand	10 pesos
Maid, per week	50–100 pesos (optional)
Doorman, hails cab	5– 10 pesos
Waiter	15%
Lavatory attendant	5 pesos
Taxi driver	10% (optional)
Filling station attendant	5 pesos
Tourist guide	optional
Woman's hairdresser	15%
Barber	15%
Theater usher	5 pesos

Movie usher	5 pesos
Shoeshine boy (total)	10–20 pesos
Gondolier (in Xochimilco)	20 pesos

TOILETS. In Mexico the toilets may be referred to as *baños, sanitarios, tocadores, escusados, retretes* or *W.C.* The doors may be labelled *caballeros* or *H (hombres)* for men and *M (mujeres)* or *damas* for women.

In public toilets attendants expect at least a token tip. In elegant establishments more is expected.

Where are the toilets?   **¿Dónde están los sanitarios?**

TOURIST INFORMATION OFFICES *(oficina de turismo)*. The Mexican government maintains many tourist information offices abroad; in addition, any Mexican consulate will provide information about travel to Mexico.

Canada:

Mexican National Tourist Council, 700 West Georgia St., Vancouver V7Y 1B6, B.C.; tel. (604) 682-0551

Mexican National Tourist Council, Suite 1212, 101 Richmond St. W., Toronto 110, Ont.; tel. 364-2455

Mexican National Tourist Council, Suite 2409, 1 Place Ville Marie, Montreal H3B 3M9, Que.; tel. (514) 871-1052

England:

Mexican National Tourist Council, 52, Grosvenor Gardens, London, SW1W OAX; tel. (01) 730-0128/9

U.S.A.:

Mexican National Tourist Council, 229 Peachtree St., N.E., Atlanta, Ga. 30303; tel. (404) 659-2409

Mexican National Tourist Council, John Hancock Center, Suite 3615, Chicago, Ill. 60611; tel. (312) 649-0090

Mexican National Tourist Council, 9701 Wilshire Blvd., Los Angeles, Calif. 90212; tel. (213) 274-6315

T Mexican National Tourist Council, 405 Park Avenue, Suite 1002, New York, N.Y. 10022; tel. (212) 755-7212

In Mexico City you can contact the Mexican Secretariat of Tourism Office *(Secretaría de Turismo)* at

Avenida Presidente Masaryk 172, México 5, D.F.; tel. 250-86-09.

Tourists can also obtain assistance and information by calling 250-01-23 in Mexico City.

W **WATER** *(agua)*. Top hotels and restaurants automatically provide purified water. Never drink water from the tap. Bottled Mexican mineral water, naturally carbonated, is pure and delicious. Bottled or canned soft drinks and juices are always safe to drink.

a bottle of mineral water	**una botella de agua mineral**
carbonated	**con gas**
non-carbonated	**sin gas**

NUMBERS

0	**cero**	18	**dicciocho**
1	**uno**	19	**diecinueve**
2	**dos**	20	**veinte**
3	**tres**	21	**veintiuno**
4	**cuatro**	22	**veintidós**
5	**cinco**	30	**treinta**
6	**seis**	31	**treinta y uno**
7	**siete**	40	**cuarenta**
8	**ocho**	50	**cincuenta**
9	**nueve**	60	**sesenta**
10	**diez**	70	**setenta**
11	**once**	80	**ochenta**
12	**doce**	90	**noventa**
13	**trece**	100	**cien**
14	**catorce**	101	**ciento uno**
15	**quince**	102	**ciento dos**
16	**dieciséis**	500	**quinientos**
17	**diecisiete**	1,000	**mil**

124

DAYS OF THE WEEK

Sunday	domingo	Wednesday	miércoles
Monday	lunes	Thursday	jueves
Tuesday	martes	Friday	viernes
		Saturday	sábado

SOME USEFUL EXPRESSIONS

yes/no	sí/no
please/thank you	por favor/gracias
excuse me/you're welcome	perdone/de nada
where/when/how	dónde/cuándo/cómo
how long/how far	cuánto tiempo/a qué distancia
yesterday/today/tomorrow	ayer/hoy/mañana
day/week/month/year	día/semana/mes/año
left/right	izquierda/derecha
up/down	arriba/abajo
good/bad	bueno/malo
big/small	grande/pequeño
cheap/expensive	barato/caro
hot/cold	caliente/frío
old/new	viejo/nuevo
open/closed	abierto/cerrado
Where are the toilets?	¿Dónde están los baños?
Waiter! Waitress!	¡Mesero!/¡Mesera!
I'd like...	Quisiera...
How much is that?	¿Cuánto es?
What time is it?	¿Qué hora es?
Do you speak English?	¿Habla usted inglés?
I don't understand.	No entiendo.
Please write it down.	Por favor, escríbalo.
Help me, please.	Ayúdeme, por favor.
Get a doctor—quickly!	¡Llamen a un médico, rápido!

Index

An asterisk (*) next to a page number indicates a map reference. All sites and buildings mentioned are in Mexico City; for those outside see under respective towns. For index to Practical Information, see p. 102.

127